WHY LIVE THE CHR...

". . .Clear, illuminating, and stimulating insight into the moral and ethical dilemma of acting upon one's belief in an unbelieving world. . ."

—BILL MOYERS, Educational Broadcasting Corporation

". . .Biblically faithful. . .marvelously practical. . .historically informed. . .refreshingly elemental. . .astoundingly broad in scope. . .. . his treatment of the cross may very well be the most significant section of this immensely significant book."

—FOY VALENTINE, Christian Life Commission, Southern Baptist Convention

". . .A very readable, articulate, and sensitive interpretation of the Christian life and of Christian ethics. . ."

—E. CLINTON GARDNER, Emory University

". . .Its contents are more inclusive, and its purpose is more fully systematic than most books written in the area of basic Christian ethics today."

—JAMES M. GUSTAFSON, University of Chicago

To
Robert Eaton
Best wishes for
a long and effective
ministry.
TBMaston
1 John 2:6

why
LIVE the
Christian
LIFE?

T. B. maston

publishers since 1798

THOMAS NELSON INC.
NASHVILLE / NEW YORK

Library of Congress Cataloging in Publication Data

Maston, Thomas Bufford, 1897-
  Why live the Christian life?

  Bibliography: p.
  1. Christian life—Baptist authors.   I. Title.
BV4501.2.M3677   248'.48'61   74-14797
ISBN 0-8407-5584-8

Unless otherwise indicated, all quotations of the Scriptures are from the Revised Standard Version. The following
abbreviations are used for other versions: KJV *(King James
Version);* NEB *(New English Bible);* TEV *(Today's English
Version or Good News for Modern Man);* and Wm. and Ph.
for the translations of the New Testament by Charles B.
Williams and J. B. Phillips.

CONTENTS

PART III: CONCLUSIONS CONCERNING THE CHRISTIAN LIFE

PREFACE

I have had a desire through the years to do two types of writing. One is more or less a scholarly type, which would appeal to college, university, and seminary students and teachers, along with college and seminary trained ministers. The other is a more or less popular type of writing primarily for Christian youth and laymen, along with ministers with limited formal education. The present volume attempts, to a limited degree, to combine both of these interests. It is hoped that college and seminary teachers will find it acceptable as a text or as required reading. The annotated bibliography at the close has been provided primarily for teachers and serious students.

The desire to reach more intelligent Christian youth and laymen explains some features of the book. For example, documentation has been kept to the minimum. Also, footnotes have been placed at the end of the book. It is hoped that the structure in general, with center headings only and with comparatively short sentences and paragraphs, will make the book relatively easy to read.

In preparing the questions "For Thought and Discussion," both of the above groups have been kept in mind. It is believed that they will help the layman as well as the minister to think through his position on some of the more pressing contemporary issues. The teacher will find them useful for class discussion. The question approach is used to help the reader, student or otherwise, to think through for himself his position on the issues. All of us need to develop the ability, under the guidance of the Holy Spirit, to relate or apply basic Christian concepts to our own particular life situations. This is the way of moral and spiritual maturity.

This book is one in a series projected some years ago. It was decided at that time that at least four books were needed to cover adequately the field of Christian ethics: biblical ethics, basic Christian ethics, social or applied ethics, and the history of Christian ethics. The present volume is the third to be written in the series. The books have not been produced in logical order. The first was *Christianity and World Issues* (Macmillan, 1957), a book that discusses some of the major issues in the area of Christian social ethics. It has been supplemented, to some degree, by a more recent book entitled *The Christian, the Church, and Contemporary Problems* (Word Books, 1968). *Biblical Ethics* (Word Books, 1967) surveys the ethical content of the entire Bible and includes a chapter on the Apocrypha, Pseudepigrapha, and Dead Sea Scrolls.

The present volume is in the area of basic Christian ethics. After an introductory chapter on "Man's Search for Truth," Part I, composed of four chapters, provides the foundation or rationale for an emphasis on the Christian life and its ethic. Part II, under several headings, discusses the nature of the Christian life: its motive, authority, supreme value, comprehensive ideal, and crowning virtue. There follows in Part III two conclusions concerning the Christian life: it is the way of the cross and the way of tension.

There are several more or less distinctive characteristics of the present volume. Other books on Christian ethics incorporate some of these characteristics, but it is believed that the combination of them in one volume justifies the addition of this book to the literature on Christian ethics. Some of the more evident emphases, one or two of which have been mentioned previously, are:

1. The extensive and direct use of the Scriptures. This has been done with the conviction that the Scriptures speak an abidingly relevant and authoritative word.

2. The relation of the Christian ethic to everyday Christian living. The Christian ethic is not a theory of life but a way of living, providing guidance for daily decisions.

3. There is no attempt to conform to or promote any particular theological position or ethical system or theory.

4. The book is considerably more limited in scope than many books in the field. Some excellent books combine in one volume biblical ethics, basic ethics, and applied or social ethics. The present volume is limited to basic ethics.

5. There is no effort to force the Christian life or its ethic into one descriptive term. It is too broad and complex for that. For example, the Christian ethic can be described as an ethic of love, but it can just as correctly be considered a will of God ethic.

6. The place given to the cross is a distinctive and possibly a unique emphasis. The "cross" comes nearer than any other one term describing the distinctive qualities of the genuine Christian life. The Christian ethic might correctly be called an ethic of the cross. But even this descriptive term is not entirely adequate when it stands alone. Other terms such as the covenant, the grace of God, the glory of God, the will of God, the kingdom of God, perfection, love, and others are needed to define the cross and make it come alive for the Christian in the midst of his daily decisions.

T. B. MASTON

I

INTRODUCTION:
Man's Search For Truth

Man is on a continuing search for truth. He is never completely satisfied. Each new discovery reveals new glimpses or insights into truth. In turn, each new insight beckons him to an additional search for truth. This is just as true in the area of the daily life of the Christian as it is anywhere else. This means that the search for truth should not be and is not exclusively the concern of the scientist, the philosopher, or the scholar. Each of us, regardless of our age or maturity is, consciously or unconsciously, on a constant search for truth. We seek answers to questions and solutions for problems that arise in the process of making daily decisions.

Daily Decisions and the Search

Some of the questions and problems are in the area of personal morality, others in the realm of social morality. At this stage, let us restrict ourselves to one example primarily but not exclusively in the personal area. A consideration of this problem will reveal how complex many decisions are and how diligently one needs to search for truth as he makes a decision.

Let us consider a case of pregnancy before marriage. There are many questions that may be and in most cases should be asked and answered. Should the couple marry?

Have an abortion? Or have the baby outside of marriage? If they should marry only under certain conditions, what are those conditions? Should the parents try to force a marriage? Should the minister perform the marriage ceremony? Always or only under some conditions? If it would be better for the girl to have the baby outside of marriage, why? Where can she go to have it? If she has the baby outside of marriage, should she keep it, permit her parents or some other relative to have it, or let it be adopted through regular child-placing channels? Whose welfare should be given primary consideration in making the decision: the relatives, the mother, the father, the baby? Who should have the primary responsibility in making the decision? Should the father be responsible for the expenses of the birth of the baby?

What should be the attitude of the young woman and the young man toward the experience they have had? What should be the attitude of the parents of the young man? What should be the attitude of the parents of the young woman toward her, toward the father of the child, and toward his parents? What about the church and church members? What about the attitude toward all concerned? What if the couple have married but it is generally known that the young woman was pregnant before marriage? How should they be recieved in and by the church family?

Many people are involved in making decisions, some of which are as crucial and involved as the preceding. Among these are decisions not only regarding sex before marriage but also sex outside of marriage, divorce, remarriage, smoking, drinking, drugs, participation in war, and others. Some of the more pressing contemporary social issues, some of which have noticeable personal aspects or implications are: abortion, euthanasia, pollution, urban deterioration, capital punishment, and integration of churches. Most of these and additional problems will be mentioned and some will be discussed later. Much of this will be done through questions for thought and discussion at the conclusion of the chapters.

Source of the Search

Back of the man's search for truth in relation to the immediate problems of his life is a general search for truth as such. In turn, the latter helps to explain our search for truth in the areas of everyday Christian living. Our never-ending search for truth, whether truth in general or in its application to specific situations, stems to a considerable degree from the nature of man. Created in the image of God, man has had that image marred but not totally destroyed by sin. Sin has affected every area of his life. This means, among other things, that his knowledge of truth is limited. But there is enough of the image of God retained to make man conscious of his limited insight into the truth and at the same time to create within him a restless searching for the truth.

We can be assured that as we search for God or *The Truth*, and the source of all truth, God is also searching for us. We search for the Searcher. There is a sense in which the source of man's search for truth is in God rather than in man. Certainly, the source of the image of God in man is God himself.

Goal of the Search

Men may be unconscious of the fact, but the ultimate goal of their search for truth or meaning is *the Truth* or God. In him they find the source of truth and that which gives unity to truth. It is *the Truth* that satisfies man's deepest search for truth. It was Augustine who said, "Thou madest us for Thyself, and our heart is restless, until it repose in Thee." In a very true sense, God is both the source of man's search for truth and the ultimate goal of that search.

The statement was made previously that man's search for truth will not be satisfied until he discovers *the Truth.* This discovery comes when man is brought into union with Christ. It is this experience that restores the marred image of God in man. There remains, however, a perplexing and potentially a very meaningful paradox. When one is brought into union with the resurrected Christ, his search or quest for *the Truth* or for true meaning in life is ended. But just as surely a new quest begins. This quest will continue until the end of life's journey.

Still another way of stating the same marvelous paradox is to suggest that through our union with Christ the image of God has been restored, but it is not completely restored. The full restoration will not come until the end of life when we shall awake in his likeness. Now we see through a glass darkly as in an old mirror. Then we shall see clearly. The incompleteness of the restoration of the image of God explains the continuing restlessness in the life of the child of God. There is within the serious Christian an abiding tension between the complete and the incomplete, the perfect and the imperfect, the whole and the partial. It seems that the more completely one comprehends the truth, the more conscious he is of falling short not only in his knowledge of truth but also in the appropriation and application of truth in his life. Many of us can say with Paul, "I do not understand my own actions. For I do not do what I want, but I do the very thing I hate. . . .I can will what is right, but I cannot do it" (Rom. 7:15, 18). And our experience is that these things have been distressingly true after we became Christians as well as before. In other words, the goal of our searching and striving is never fully realized or attained.

Approaches in the Search

Broadly speaking, man has made three approaches in his search for truth: the scientific, the philosophical, and the religious. Some acquaintance with these approaches can be of value and should be of interest to Christian men and women in general and not exclusively to scholars.

Generally speaking, science seeks to understand the world of nature; philosophy attempts to understand man and his place in the universe; while religion and specifically theology seek to understand God and his relation to nature and man. Science searches for truth primarily by analyzing the observable phenomena of the natural order. Philosophy uses the rational approach in its search for truth. Religion in general and theology in particular claim a unique divine revelation of truth. From the perspective of the Christian religion, an effort is made to comprehend and to interpret truth as revealed in nature and in man, but ultimately and preeminently in Christ.

Each of these approaches can properly be considered a good gift from God. Each is autonomous, to a considerable degree, but they also are closely inter-related, with each making some contributions to the other. Furthermore, since God is the source of all truth, there cannot be any real conflict between science, philosophy, and religion. When any conflict arises, it is due to incompleteness or immaturity in one or more of these areas.

The one thing that distinguishes more pointedly than anything else the approaches to truth of science but particularly of philosophy and the Christian religion is the difference in their point of reference or place of beginning. The Christian approach begins with God, the philosophical approach with man. Although both have a place for faith and reason, the Christian approach begins with faith, the philosophical with reason. The former centers on what God in

Christ has done, the latter on what man can do. A distinctly Christian approach to truth may make use of the rational, but it begins with the self-revelation of God as recorded in the Scriptures and as climaxed in his Son. While the Christian may admit the possibility of revelation in the areas of philosophy and science, he contends that Christian thought is grounded basically in a unique or special revelation of the redemptive truth of God. He also believes that although Jesus gives the answers to man's moral problems and perplexities, far more important is the fact that he *is* the answer. The Christian believes (1) that Christ has revealed in his life God's ultimate ideal for man, and (2) that man's union with the resurrected Christ creates within him the desire, the dynamic, the power to move toward God's ideal or purpose for him. This has tremendous significance for the Christian ethic and the Christian life in general.

Historically speaking, the Christian movement has been largely shaped by two streams of influence: the Jewish and the Grecian. The first represents the revelational approach to truth, the latter the philosophical or rational approach. The Jewish influence was particularly pronounced in original Christianity. Some Greek influence is seen in Paul and in John, but even they were basically Jewish in their perspective. The Grecian influence became more pronounced in post-New Testament times. Many of the early church fathers were students of Greek philosophy before their conversion to Christianity. They did not and could not leave all that influence behind.

The Christian Ethic and the Search

Now, in a more specific way, how is the Christian ethic related to man's search for truth and to the approaches he has made in that search? Ethics is clearly an integral phase of man's search for truth. And like other areas of man's knowledge of the truth, it remains incomplete with an open-endedness toward truth. This means, among other things, that Christian ethics needs the insights of philosophy and science to help fill out its knowledge of the truth and to test and clarify its interpretation of revealed truth.

Also, the various approaches to truth interpenetrate one another in the search for truth in the area of moral decisions as well as in other areas. One's emphasis in the search for truth will determine, to a considerable degree, the place of science, philosophy, and religion in the search. From the viewpoint of moral decisions, if one's emphasis is primarily on basic concepts, ideas, or principles, then philosophy and/or theology will have a major place in his search for truth. In contrast, the greater one's interest in the application of truth to particular problems and situations the more important will be the sciences and particularly social sciences. For example, in a very real sense, Christian social or applied ethics is a middle discipline, standing between theology and the social sciences. Those who work in the area look to theology for their basic stance and to the social sciences for factual knowledge concerning social problems and for an understanding of the structures and techniques that will help them to apply Christian principles more effectively to the problems of the world. For example, Christians in their attempt to speak effectively to such contemporary problems as abortion, race relations, unemployment, war, and peace are heavily indebted to and dependent upon the social sciences such as psychology and sociology.

Christian Ethics, Theology, and the Search

The Christian in the pew as well as the pulpit has a theology and also an ethic. His basic ideas concerning God, man, sin, salvation, and related theological concepts, along with his ideas concerning right and wrong, will be determining factors in his daily decisions. The two, theology and ethics, are closely related in our search for truth. They are both basically revelational in approach. The ultimate goal of the search in both areas is the same: the knowledge of *the truth*. Both are grounded in the will and nature of God. They belong together. They represent two sides of the same coin. In the Scriptures and in the early church period, with rare exceptions, they were not clearly separated.

In spite of the close relation of theology and ethics, it should be recognized that they, to some degree, are distinct and supplement one another. Ethics looks back to theology; theology looks forward to ethics. Theology provides the foundation; ethics builds the superstructure on the foundation. Both are essential for the completion of the building. When we say that theology is the foundation, it does not mean that theology is divorced from life. As John Calvin said, "Doctrine is not an affair of the tongue, but of the life." He insisted that "it must be transfused into the breast, and pass into the conduct, and so transform us into itself."[1]

The consideration of Christian ethics as a separate discipline is justified in the contemporary period. This is true because of the prevalence and complexity of modern moral and social problems. A separate emphasis on Christian ethics is also justified because of the tendency to neglect it. Furthermore, when theologians speak in the area of everyday Christian living, many of them tend to be too exclusively theoretical and speculative. In contrast, the Christian ethicist, even when he is most theoretical, has or should have a major interest in the application of theory to actual life situations. In conclusion, Christian ethics should acknowledge its close relation and its indebtedness to theology, but at the same time it should insist that it has a distinctive emphasis and contribution to make to the Christian life.

Christian Ethics, Philosophical Ethics, and the Search

Christian ethics and philosophical ethics represent, to a considerable degree, distinctive approaches in man's search for truth. Philosophical ethics uses the rational approach, while a distinctly Christian ethic begins with a unique revelation of truth. In the former, the search is for truth; in the latter, the search is for an understanding of truth that has been given or revealed. The division, however, between philosophical and Christian ethics should not be drawn too sharply. Each has its own distinctive contribution to make. Each can enrich the other. And after all, our sovereign God is concerned for the totality of life, which means that he may be concerned about and active in the area of philosophical ethics as well as in the area of Christian ethics.

Although we believe that philosophical ethics can make some distinctive contibutions to our knowledge of ethics, we do think that Christian and philosophical ethics differ in many and important respects. The distinctive elements of the Christian ethic stem from the fact that it is centered in God rather than in man. For example, the supreme value, from the perspective or philosophical ethics, is always grounded in or directed toward man. It is pleasure, wisdom, or pure contemplation. In contrast, the supreme good or value in the Christian ethic is centered in God. It is the promotion of the kingdom of God.

Likewise, the source of authority differs in the two. In philosophical ethics, it centers in man: his reason or his conscience. In Christian ethics, it centers in God and his will. Reason or the rational nature may and should be used in the Christian's search for the will of God, but reason is a means or instrument in the search and not its end. And since there is perfect harmony in God, the will of God is expressive of and evolves from his nature. This means that authority for the child of God ultimately rests in the nature of God.

A distinctive aspect of the Christian ethic is the fact that it, through the faith on which it is grounded, has an answer for sin, which is man's basic problem. The grace of God provides the remedy for man's sin. This gives to the Christian a deep and unique sense of responsibility. This means, contrary to the position of some contemporary situationalists, that there is an important place for a sense of obligation or the imperative in the Christian ethic. However, in the Christian ethic as in the Christian life in general, the imperative is preceded by the indicative, oughtness by isness. An obligation is placed upon us by what God, through his grace, has done for us.

Ours is an ethic of grace, a grace that first speaks to us in the indicative mood but then speaks just as surely in the imperative mood. Really, these two, the indicative and the imperative, alternate; there is a constant interplay of the two. It could not be otherwise because of the dynamic nature of the Christian faith. It is never static; there is constant movement. This involves a movement from the indicative to the imperative followed by a movement back to pick up a new indicative or at least a deepened insight into the indicative.

The ethic of the grace or goodness of God also provides a distinctive dynamic or motivation. The Christian, through his union with the resurrected Christ, has a deep inner desire to show by the quality of life he lives his appreciation for what God has done for him. He also discovers that he moves toward the purposes of God in his life as he permits the resurrected Christ to live in him and express himself through him. That which was a potentiality in the initial experience we had with the Lord should be permitted to become a living, dynamic reality in our lives. The movement of the Christian life is from within outward. In other words, the Christian ethic, as it finds expression in daily Christian living, is not something put on from the outside;

it is something that naturally and inevitably evolves from an inner relationship. The ultimate ideal for the Christian is a complete harmony between the inner and the outer, between what the Christian does and what he wants to do.

Christian Ethics and the Christian Life

Christian ethics is basically an attempt to study and interpret the Christian life. It may become largely an intellectual exercise restricted primarily to the academic community. This may not be particularly damaging in a period of relative stability. It is most unfortunate, however, for ethics to be divorced from daily life and problems in a time of world revolution such as the contemporary period. If Christian ethics is to be relevant to and a vital factor in the life of the world, it must move out where people live. There is some question whether ethics in general and Christian ethics in particular can separate itself from life. The decisions and problems of the world and the peoples of the world provide the content of ethics. In turn, the more perplexing and pressing the problems of life, the more important it is for all of us in pew and pulpit, in schoolroom and sanctuary, to study Christian ethics.

Christian ethics may be defined as critical reflection on the moral decisions and actions of individual Christians and of the Christian community. Christian ethics performs both an analytical and a prescriptive function, with the former preceding the latter. These two, the analytical and prescriptive, are closely related to the indicative and the imperative, mentioned previously. It makes little difference which of these is considered most important, just so it is recognized that there is a place for both.

The analytical and prescriptive functions are not as sharply differentiated as some seem to think. When Christian ethics is primarily analytical, the prescriptive element is present, at least to a tentative degree, as a basis for the analysis. John Bennett's relatively well-known definition of Christian ethics could be interpreted from either the analytical or prescriptive perspective. He says, "Christian ethics is the name given to the attempt to think through the implications of Christian faith for the moral life." While the analytical element is primary in this definition—"to think through"—yet a prescriptive or imperative element is present. For there to be any "implications of the Christian faith for the moral life," "the Christian faith" and "the moral life" would have to have some tangible content.

For Lehmann, Christian ethics "*is the reflection upon the question, and its answer: What am I, as a believer in Jesus Christ and as a member of his church, to do?*" [2] Again, let us suggest that one has to know something about the kind or quality of life "a believer in Jesus Christ" will or should live, if he is to know what to do. One must know what and who he is if he is to know what to do. One may scrupulously avoid the words "ought" and "should", but there is present an element of obligation whatever may be one's approach to Christian ethics and to the Christian life.

Christian ethics and the Christian's daily life interact on one another. There are abiding values in the historic content of the Christian ethic, but it is constantly in the process of reformulation because of the changing experiences and problems of people. What a theology teacher of mine said about theology could also be said concerning the Christian ethic. His statement was: "Every generation needs to rewrite its theology." This must be true, to some degree, of the Christian ethic if it is to meet the needs of changing situations. This means that the Christian ethic, at any particular point in time, is a product, to some degree, of Christian experience. The preceding statement does not necessitate the elimination of or even the diminution of the importance of certain basic moral concepts or principles of our Christian faith. It does suggest a fresh interpretation of those concepts and new insights into their application to daily Christian living. It also means that the formulation of the Christian ethic at any particular time is provisional in some ways and to some degree. Room must be left for new insights in the light of changing situations.

As implied in the preceding, the provisional nature of the Christian ethic at any particular time stems not only from the contemporary situation but also from the nature of the Christian ethic and the Christian faith. The Christian faith, with its ethic, is beyond the complete comprehension of man. He is constantly discovering new facets and getting a deeper understanding of his faith and its ethic. Some of these insights are the result of man's attempt to apply what he knows to the changing problems and challenges of his life.

FOR THOUGHT AND DISCUSSION

1. There are three theories or groups of theories concerning the relation of philosophical ethics and Christian ethics: elimination, absorption, and supplemental. Which would most nearly express your position?
2. James Gustafson formerly of Yale now at the University of Chicago has written concerning what he has called "a misplaced debate in Christian ethics" (Martin E. Marty and Dean G. Peerman, eds., *New Theology* #3, p. 70). He suggests that there are four points from which Christian ethicists start in working out their system of ethics. Those points are: (1) the situation, (2) certain fundamental theological affirmations, (3) certain moral principles, and (4) the nature of the Christian life in Christ and its proper expression in moral conduct.

Gustafson further suggests that wherever one starts he moves in the direction of the others. Do you think the latter statement is correct? Which of the four approaches would come nearest stating your position? It has been suggested that the Bible should be a fifth beginning point. Would you agree?

3. A considerable search is on in the contemporary period regarding the use and the effects of drugs. There are rather sharp differences of opinion about marijuana, its effects, and the attitude society should have toward it. Some people contend that it is no more harmful than alcohol, and its sale and use should be legalized. Others suggest that if not legalized the penalties for possession and use should be reduced. What do you think? How prevalent is the use of alcohol, LSD, heroin, and other drugs by those you know? What are the most effective approaches in counteracting the drug menace? What can parents do? schools? churches?

PART ONE
FOUNDATIONS FOR THE
CHRISTIAN LIFE

The chapters of Part One seek to provide a foundation, basis, or rationale for an emphasis on everyday Christian living. A distinctly Christian ethic and a distinctly Christian approach to life in general logically begin with God (Chapter II), have an important place for man (Chapter III), are grounded in the biblical revelation (Chapter IV), and naturally evolve from the Christian's experience in and with the resurrected Christ (Chapter V).

II

THE NATURE OF GOD

What W. S. Bruce said some years ago about Old Testament morality could be said concerning the Christian life in general. He said that Old Testament morality revolved around God as the earth revolves around the sun. So it is or should be with the Christian life. God should be the final point of reference in all that the child of God does.

What is there in the nature of the God around whom the Christian life revolves that will provide a ground or rationale for an emphasis on everyday Christian living? What is there about God that will give us guidelines as we seek to know the kind of life we should live?

Revealed and Concealed

A logical place to begin a study of the nature of God is the fact that he has sought through the centuries to reveal himself, his character, and his will to man. Men, however, have been limited in their capacity to receive, appropriate, or understand that revelation. Finally he sent his Son as the full revelation of the Father. However, the men who were most closely associated with the Son were unable to comprehend fully all that he sought to reveal to them concerning the Father. He himself said that the Holy Spirit, when he came, would give them additional insights into the truth. The Divine Spirit has continued to seek to lead the children of God into a clearer understanding of the nature and will of God.

But at best, what we comprehend now is like "puzzling

reflections in a mirror" (NEB) or "the baffling reflection of reality" (Ph.). At present all we know "is a little fraction of the truth." There will come a time, however, when we will know fully (1 Cor. 13:12).

Augustine expressed the paradoxical nature of our knowledge of God when he spoke of God as the "most High, and the most near; most secret, and most present." [1] To use traditional theological terms, God is both transcendent and imminent. Bonhoeffer says that "God is the 'Beyond' in the midst of our life." [2] He is known and yet unknown. He is the other, but not the "wholly other." He is secret and yet present.

In Christ we have found God, and yet we have not found him completely. We have the assurance that he exists, and yet we continue to search for him. He has been revealed to us, but he is still concealed from us. It really seems that the more fully he has been revealed the more completely he seems to be concealed. The hunger that is satisfied when we find him in turn creates a renewed or a deeper hunger for a fuller knowledge of him and his will for us and for our world. The more mature we become in him and hence the better we know him the more conscious we become of how limited our knowledge is of him.

The preceding is the major source for a deep-seated tension in the life of the sincere, seeking child of God. It is the kind of tension that keeps one's face set toward the sunrise of new insights and additional light. It is the type of tension that is necessary if progress is to be made in one's understanding of God and his will for our lives.

As we search for a deeper and clearer understanding of the nature and will of God, we can be assured that he is seeking to reveal himself and his will to us. We are seeking him because he has already sought and found us. There is a very real sense in which we seek the Seeker. The question he asked Adam in the Garden is one that he continues to ask man, "Where are you?" (Gen. 3:9). Where are we? Are we trying to hide from him or are we searching for him? Where are we in our knowledge of him? Where are we in obedience to his will? Where are we in our likeness to him? How fully do we reveal him to others? Where are we?

A Moral Person

Just as it is assumed in the Scriptures that God exists, so it is assumed that he is a Person. All the qualities associated with a person are attributed to him. When we say that God is a person and when we ascribe personal qualities to him, we are using human language in an attempt to understand God and to describe to others what we believe we know about him. The words used to describe God, including the word Person, to use an expression of Luther, need to be "given a bath." They need to be cleansed of their association with the human person.

It should be remembered, however, that language is not static. There may be continuity in the use of words, but there is also movement. For example, when words are related to new objects, they take on new meaning. This is true of a word like "person." It is a human word, but when applied to God new life is breathed into it. God fills the word to the full as he does every word that is applied to him. This is one reason for man's inability to comprehend fully the nature of God. One never even fully understands another human person. This is true in the most intimate human relationship, that of husband and wife. They never completely understand one another.

The fact that God is a person has tremendous significance for our relations with him and everyday Christian living. For one thing, the fact the he is a person means that to be right in our relations to him we must be right on a personal basis.

Although a human illustration is an inadequate tool to

express a great spiritual or divine truth, let us use the relation of husband and wife to illustrate our relation to God as a person. A husband may pride himself on his generous provisions for his wife and his thoughtfulness concerning special occasions. He may think that these things are all his wife should expect. These things are commendable, if they are not made substitutes for something deeper and more meaningful. Many a wife, however, has said, and also some husbands, "It is not primarily your gifts I want, I want you." She is a person, a Thou, and her husband cannot be right with her unless he is right on a personal basis.

So it is with our relation to God. He is a person. Unless we are right with him on a personal basis, we are not acceptable to him and will not be approved by him. This means, among other things, that to be right with God involves more than faithfulness to the formalities of our faith, more than orthodoxy of belief, freedom from hurtful habits, or even active participation in the work of the Lord. There is a dimension to our relation to God as a person that goes deeper than any of the preceding.

There are many Christians who evidently think they can please God by attending worship services regularly, giving a tithe of their income, and being active in the work of the church. Many of us, if we listen, may hear our heavenly Father say, "These you ought to have done, without neglecting the weightier more important matters" (see Matt. 23:23). Formalities are poor and inadequate substitutes for the vitalities of our faith.

There are abundant evidences or proofs in the Scripture that God is a moral person. Really to be a person involves a sense of moral values and responsibility. There are places, however, where specific moral qualities are directly attributed to God; he is just (Ezra 9:15; Ps. 145:17), the Just One (Acts 22:14), righteous (Ps. 7:9; 11:7; 119:137; 129:4), and the "holy and righteous One" (Acts 3:4).

These and other qualities are also revealed in the way

God acted or acts. He is just because he is "just in all his ways" (Ps. 145:7). He is righteous because he is "righteous in all the works which he has done" (Dan. 9:14). He judges righteously (Jer. 11:20), his acts are righteous (1 Sam. 12:7), and his judgments are just (Rev. 16:5, 7).

There are a number of other moral traits or attributes of God. One of the most meaningful is love, which will be discussed in a later chapter. We shall limit the discussion in this section to brief statements concerning God's faithfulness or dependability and his holiness. The former is frequently neglected, while the latter is as comprehensive as any one character trait of God.

The faithfulness or dependability of God is a major theme of the Bible. It is related in a particular way to his covenant relation with his people. He is not only a covenant-making God, he is also a covenant-keeping God. His faithfulness to his covenant with his people places them under obligation to keep the covenant.

God's dependability is also evident in the natural order and in the moral order. It is well to remember that the basic laws of God, natural and moral, are unchanging. They are written into the nature of man and of the world in which he lives.

Of the attributes of God none is more inclusive than his holiness. In the main, it is related, as is true of his dependability, to and is expressive of his covenant relation to his people. The latter are a holy people separated from the world and separated unto their God and to his purposes. The "from" and "unto" represent the negative and positive aspects of holiness.

There is at least one other thing that should be said concerning the moral attributes of God. They are not sharply divided. They merge into one another. There is unity in the person of God. For example, there is not wrath on the one hand and love on the other. His wrath is expressive of his love. Also, his love is both holy and righteous. The reverse can also be said. Righteousness must be expressive of and in a sense must incorporate love if it is to be the righteousness of God.

One thing that explains the unity in the person of God is the fact that the attributes of God are not external to him. They naturally evolve from his nature as a moral person. There is a real sense in which every attribute or character trait is the expression of the essence of God. God is not only "light" (1 John 1:5) and "love" (1 John 4:8, 16), he is also "grace," "righteousness," "faithfulness," and "holiness."

There is at least one other factor that helps to explain the unity in the person of God. Every character trait properly attributed to God finds perfect expression in him. He is perfect love, complete righteousness, undiluted faithfulness, and untarnished holiness. When these qualities are raised to the level of perfection, there can be no conflict in them.

The perfection of every moral trait of God is most completely revealed in the cross. What John says about love could be said concerning every other attribute. His statement is, "By this we know love ["what love is" NEB], that he laid down his life for us" (1 John 3:16). We could never have known the depth of God's love *(agape)* apart from Christ's death on the cross. Likewise, we could never have known the full meaning of God's grace, mercy, righteousness, or holiness apart from the cross.

The preceding has considerable significance for the children of God. We should have a deepening desire that our lives will increasingly express the same character traits found in God and that these traits will be the expression of a unified or integrated personality. This will be true as and to the degree that the outer expressions of our lives are the normal, natural expressions of the inner life. In other words, to the degree that love, mercy, justice, faithfulness, holiness and other traits have become a part of the very essence of our being, to that degree they will be the outer expressions of a well-integrated personality.

In turn, these traits will become the normal, the natural, the inevitable expression of our lives to the degree that we let the resurrected Christ live in us and express himself through us. In other words, they will evolve from a vital inner relation with the Person who has all these qualities to the level of perfection.

Furthermore, the more completely we appropriate the deeper meaning of the cross the more we will reveal to others the basic moral character of God. They will see at least to a limited degree revealed in our lives the love, grace, righteousness, faithfulness, and holiness of God. As we take up our cross and follow him they will see him and understand something of our relation to him.

Sovereign

A scientist has said, "We have found a strange footprint on the shores of the unknown." The child of God believes that the footprint has been left by the sovereign God of the universe. His creative power brought the universe into existence. His creative work, however, is not restricted to the past. He is now creatively active in the world, seeking to work out his will and purpose. Jesus said on one occasion, "My Father is working still, and I am working" (John 5:17). Since God is active in the contemporary world, he can be encountered existentially by a child of his in the changing situations of life.

The concern of the sovereign God is as broad as life. He is not only concerned about every aspect of the life of the individual; he is also interested in the welfare of society and is active in the affairs of the nations of the world. He could not be sovereign unless his sovereignty was inclusive of all of life. As sovereign he is at work in the schoolroom and in the legislative hall as well as in the sanctuary. He is seeking to work out his purposes in and through the civic club, the fraternal order, the labor union, and the chamber of commerce as well as in and through the church. He is active in the science laboratory and the philosopher's study as well as in the halls of the theological seminary. In some areas of life, to use an expression of Kierkegaard's, God may be, from our perspective, "incognito." We may not be conscious of his presence, but we can be sure that he is there. If we think of history as a great drama, God is not only the author of the script and director of the play, he is also the chief actor and participant in the drama.

Our God is the God of every man, of every nation, and of every aspect of every life. This perspective concerning God and his sovereignty is "whole-istic." As children of God we should be "whole-istic" in our approach to life. We should have a deep sense of responsibility to God for the totality of life. There is no decision that we make and no problem that we face that is beyond the range of the concern of our heavenly Father. This is true of problems as widely divergent as liquor-by-the-drink, smoking, homosexuality, guaranteed annual income, and Bible reading and prayer in the public school.

Furthermore, since we serve the sovereign God we can go to our task with hope rather than despair, with a sense of ultimate victory rather than of defeat. We can face the world and whatever opposition we may find in it with chin up. We know that the final word belongs to our God. The clearest evidence of this fact is the empty tomb. It speaks the word of victory over all the forces that oppose the purposes of God.

Father

The God who is the sovereign God of the universe is also our heavenly Father. Here again we are forced to use human language to express a divine relationship. As is true of every human term applied to God, its association with him breathes new life and meaning into the term. The human father on the highest level is a very imperfect representation of God as father. There is a continuing challenge to human fathers to move toward the full expression of the concept in the fatherhood of God.

While the idea of God as father is much more prevalent in the New Testament than in the Old Testament, there are a number of such references in the latter (see Deut. 32:6; Isa. 63:1b; Jer. 3:19). In the New Testament there are approximately 275 references to God as Father, with over 100 of these in John's gospel and an additional dozen in 1 John. It is primarily the Johannine writings that have made "Father" the more or less natural name for God for Christians, although it is used in the synoptic gospels and frequently in Paul's epistles.

One reason for the prevalence of "Father" as a name for God in the New Testament is the fact that Jesus so frequently used the term. Many of the references of Jesus to God as Father were simply to "the Father." Being conscious of a unique relation to God, he frequently referred to God as "my Father." He also used the expression "your Father," with nineteen such references in Matthew's gospel, with fifteen of these in the Sermon on the Mount and all but four of them in chapter six.

It was in the Model Prayer that Jesus used the all-inclusive "Our Father." If God is "my Father" and "your Father," then he is "our Father." The "our" of the original prayer included Jesus and his disciples. Today it includes all who have come into the family of God through their union with the resurrected Christ. The "our Father" makes prayer drastically and for some embarrassingly inclusive. It presents a tremendous challenge to the children of God. Can we pray "our Father" with all of God's children: with those of other churches and denominations, with those of other classes and castes, with those of other colors and races? We should remember that the God who is the father of all of his children cannot really be "my Father" unless I can accept him as "your Father" and hence as "our Father."

It possibly should be added that although God is in the proper and deepest sense only the father of those who have come into his spiritual family, nevertheless he has a fatherly attitude toward all men. He makes his sun to rise "on the evil and the good and sends rain on the just and the unjust" (Matt. 5:45). This means that we, his children, should have a brotherly attitude toward all men, even toward those who are not our spiritual brothers.

What was the image that Jesus sought to give when he used "Father" to describe God? One thing that he beautifully portrayed in the Sermon on the Mount is the fact that the Father knows our needs and has resources to provide for those needs. Because of his fatherly care we are not to worry or be anxious about what we shall eat, drink, or wear. Our Father knows that we have need of these things. We are to seek first his kingdom and his righteousness with the calm assurance that the necessities of life will be provided for us.

God as Father is concerned about his children as individuals. How glorious to remember that the sovereign God of the universe knows us by name. We are not mere dots in space, not mere numbers in a computerized world; we are persons, not "its" but "thous." Frequently in the Scriptures persons are addressed by name: "Moses," (Exod. 3:4), "Elijah" (1 Kings 19:9, 13), "Samuel" (1 Sam. 3:10). Jesus, the good or true shepherd, knows his sheep by name and they recognize his voice and follow him (John 10:3, 4, 14).

It may be wise to remind ourselves that we are not by nature sons or children of God. Our sonship is by adoption (see Rom. 8:15, 23; 9:4; Gal. 4:5; Eph. 1:5). Through our union with Christ we are brought not only into the formal status of children, but there is also created within us a new heart with new motives and purposes. It is this experience that causes us to cry out "Abba! Father!" (Rom. 8:15; cf. Mark 14:36). Paul used another figure, applying it particularly to the Gentiles, which portrays our relation to God. Paul suggested that the Gentiles, a wild olive shoot, had been grafted into a cultivated olive tree (Rom. 11:17, 19, 23, 24). We have been grafted into Christ.

Whatever figure or symbol we may use to portray our relation to God as Father, the relation entails responsibility on our part. The father in the days of Jesus was the authoritative figure in the home. The will, the rule, the reign of our heavenly Father is to be supreme. As sons and daughters of the sovereign God, who is our Father, we are obligated to seek his will and, once knowing it, we are to be obedient to it. We are to put his cause, his kingdom first in our lives. Every privilege we have as children of God increases our obligation to live a life worthy of his blessings and of being recognized as a member of his family.

It was Calvin who said: "Ever since God exhibited himself to us as a Father, we must be convicted of extreme ingratitude if we do not in turn exhibit ourselves as his sons. . .Ever since he ingrafted us into his body, we, who are his members, should anxiously beware of contracting any stain or taint." [3]

The Kinship Appeal

The kinship appeal is a prominent motif in the Scriptures. For example, God said that the children of Israel were to be kind and helpful to widows, orphans, and sojourners among them not only because he had been kind to the children of Israel but also because he had a special concern for the neglected and underprivileged (see Deut. 10:18–19; 24:17). Occasionally God says in a specific way that his people are to be like him. An example is the frequently quoted statement: "You shall be holy; for I the Lord your God am holy" (Lev. 19:2; cf. 11:44).

Over and over again the children of Israel were admonished to walk in the way of the Lord (a few of many references are: Deut. 5:33; 8:6; 10:12; Josh. 22:5; Jer. 7:23), which means basically an obedience to his commandments. His commandments, however, are expressive of his nature and hence to walk in the way of the Lord in the final analysis means to walk as he walks, to be like him. God reveals himself and his character by his relation to the peoples of the world, by the way he treats them. In the same way, his children will reveal their kinship to him by the way they relate themselves to people.

The kinship appeal is clearly evident in the New Testament. For example, Jesus admonished his disciples to love their enemies and gave as a motive that they might be sons of their father (Matt. 5:45). He then adds the continually challenging admonition or ideal: "You, therefore, must be perfect as your heavenly Father is perfect" (Matt. 5:48).

Paul used the example of Jesus as a basis for his appeal to the Corinthian church for a liberal offering for the saints at Jerusalem (2 Cor. 8:1–9). In discussing what was evidently a rather prevalent problem regarding the eating of meat offered to idols, he appealed to the strong or mature not to please themselves but to please their neighbors. He gave as a motive the fact that Christ did not please himself. In other words, Christ set the example; his disciples should be like him (see Rom. 15:1–3). To the Ephesians he wrote: "Walk (*peripateo*—literally "walk around," frequently translated "live") in love, as Christ loved us and gave himself up for us" (Eph. 5:2). He exhorted the Philippians to have the same mind or attitude of humility that was found in Jesus (Phil. 2:5–8). The Colossians were asked to forgive one another as Christ had forgiven them (Col. 3:13; cf. Eph. 4:32).

The initial and continuing invitation of Jesus was and is "Follow me" (Mark 1:17; 2:14; 10:21; Matt. 16:24). To be a disciple of his is to walk in his way, to follow where he leads. He did not and does not give detailed instructions about the way in which we should walk. The best instructions come from examining the life he lived. He never asked a disciple of his to walk in a way that he had not walked and will not walk with him. We should remember, however, that his teachings, including his teachings by example as well as by word of mouth, provide a compass rather than a road map. That compass points to an open road and deepening fellowship with him as we walk with him in the way.

If we walk with him, we will have a deep interest in people—in all kinds of people but particularly in the common people, the neglected, the social and moral outcasts of our society. We shall have compassion for the masses of humanity who are harrassed and helpless like sheep without a shepherd (Matt. 9:36; cf. 14:14; 15:32), but we shall also have compassion on individuals who suffer (see Matt. 20:30–34; Mark 1:40–42; Luke 7:11–15). In other words, our compassion will be individualized or personalized as well as generalized. If we walk in the way with him we, like him, will go about doing good (Acts 10:38) and the good we do will naturally and inevitably result from the vitality of our relationship to him.

The preceding represents a goal far beyond our hope of attainment in this life. In the meantime, to use a Pauline expression, we should "as God's dear children, try to be like him" (Eph. 5:1 NEB). To be like him means perfection and Paul frankly says, "I have not yet reached perfection" but he then adds, "but I press on hoping to take hold of that for which Christ once took hold of me" (Phil. 3:12 NEB). The goal of Paul's life was not behind him; it was constantly before him. Here is a major source of the tension in the life of the child of God that assures progress toward the goal. We can be assured that our heavenly Father will be very understanding and forgiving about our failure to measure up fully to his purpose for our lives if we strive honestly and sincerely to move toward his ideal for us. It seems that he judges us more by the direction of our lives than by our present level of living. Are our faces set toward the open road of additional insight into his will and way and to a renewed dedication to his ultimate goal for our lives?

Let us also not forget that he is the main source of strength to help us move in the direction he would have us to go. The Divine Spirit is given to walk by our side, or better, to live within us and to give us the desire, the dynamic, and at the same time the power to move more and more toward the purposes of our heavenly Father in and for our lives.

FOR THOUGHT AND DISCUSSION

1. How can a Christian witness effectively where he lives, works, and plays? What about in the fraternity or sorority? The chamber of commerce or the labor union? The civic club or the fraternal order?

2. It has been suggested that one basis for the contemporary dissatisfaction of many people, particularly youth, is the tendency toward depersonalization in our socie-

ty. People are frequently treated, so it is claimed, as mere numbers rather than persons. How much validity is there to this contention? How would a proper understanding of the nature of God and of his attitude toward man help with this problem?

3. One of the most acute problems of the contemporary period is pollution: land, water, noise, and air. How would a comprehensive perspective concerning Christian stewardship relate to this problem and its solution? In turn, how is a proper or inclusive conception of stewardship related to the nature of God, particularly his sovereignty? How is the following statement related to the preceding: "Pollution is basically a theological problem"?

III
THE NATURE OF MAN

As a foundation for the Christian life, one's doctrine of man is exceeded in importance only by his doctrine of God. And these two doctrines are closely interrelated. For example, man cannot be understood apart from his relation to God. Ultimately God alone knows what man is and he alone can reveal man to himself.

Wholeness

One of the most basic aspects of that revelation is that man is an indivisible whole. We may think of him as a body or as a soul or spirit, but these two—body and soul—belong together. These aspects of man's being are like two sides of a coin. On one side, the body, man is identified with nature and is subject to the physical and psychological laws of the natural order. His life is a "running toward death." On the other side of his being, he is related to the eternal or immaterial world. While running toward death he, at least potentially, is also running toward life in its fulness.

As a spiritual being, man is capable of standing above and apart from nature. This capacity distinguishes man, so far as we know, from all the remainder of God's creation. This is one source of his "grandeur." On the other hand, the fact that he can never completely escape his relatedness to the natural order is a source of many of his problems and perplexities.

There is something within man that causes him to reach for the stars, but at the same time he finds that his feet are set in the concrete of his own physical nature. To change the figure, man has one foot solidly planted on the earth and the other at least lifted in the direction of the eternal. He is a "child of earth" and of "the starry heaven," a curious compound of "stardust and common clay."

The preceding suggests that man is an antithesis, but in the deepest sense he is a synthesis. There may seem to be a conflict between his body and his spirit, between his reach and his grasp, but these are blended into one person. This one person may not be perfectly unified; his wholeness may be incomplete; it may remain a potentiality rather than a reality, but at least deep within him there is a hunger or an outreach for wholeness.

Man's failure to attain perfect wholeness or completeness stems not only from his finiteness but also from his sinfulness. Sin separates him from God, the only perfectly whole Person. Even after he has come into the spiritual family of God through his union with Christ, man is still plagued with his sinful nature. His conflict with God and within himself is not entirely eliminated.

Some people have sought to read a thoroughgoing dualism into Paul's view of man. Paul speaks of a conflict between the flesh and the spirit (see Romans 8). It seems clear, however, that "flesh" for Paul does not mean the body as such. Rather, it refers to the fleshly or carnal nature which is in conflict with the spiritual nature. This is an inner conflict that affects the total person.

For Paul, and from the Christian perspective in general, the total person by nature is in rebellion against God. In this sense, we can properly speak of the total depravity of man. It does not mean that man is as depraved as he can be; it simply means that man as a person, spirit or soul as well as body, is depraved or is affected by sin. In other words, man the person cannot be compartmentalized for the assessment of responsibility for sin. This also means that when man, through union with Christ, becomes a new creature in Christ Jesus, the total man is saved. In other words, the "souls" of men are not saved, men as persons are saved. Just as the total person is involved in sin, so the total person is involved in salvation from the power and penalty of sin.

A mistake made by many who seek to relieve some human need or solve some basic human problem is the compartmentalization of the lives of men. Frequently an effort is made to minister to their physical, mental, or spiritual needs without a proper regard for the other needs of their lives. Man is a person, and if he is to be ministered to most effectively, he must be ministered to as a total person and not as a body or a soul.

Image of God

No concept concerning man is more significant for human relations and for the Christian life in general than the fact that man was created in the image or likeness of God. It is the image of God in man that makes him a "thou" instead of an "it," one who counts rather than one to be counted, one who has a name rather than a mere number.

What is meant when it says that man was created in the image of God? Basically it means that since God is a Person, man is a person. A person can say to himself, "I am, I ought, I will." In other words, a person has a sense of self-consciousness, a conviction of moral responsibility, and the capacity of self-determination.

No one idea is more central in the concept of the image than the fact that inherent in the image is a call or a summons to communicate with other persons. There is no person without other persons. It is no mere accident that Robinson Crusoe was a fictitious character, and even he had his man Friday. Man cannot find fulfillment for that which is basic in his nature without other persons. On the highest level, he finds this fulfillment in communion with God. Man alone of God's created beings has the capacity for an I-Thou relation not only with his fellowman but also with God. He has the ability to respond to God's self-disclosure or self-communication. Also, consciously or unconsciously, he has a deep hunger for such communication.

Another perspective concerning the meaning of the image of God in man is that man was created as God's representative in the world. Human monarchs set up images of themselves in their kingdoms. God has set man in the world as his image, a live rather than a dead image. As the representative of God, man is a symbol of God's presence in the world. Unfortunately, man too frequently has exalted himself to the place that properly belongs to God, and at times he has attempted to create God in his image. However, when man does that, he ultimately debases rather than exalts himself. The thing that gives man his real stature and standing is his relatedness to God.

As God's representative in the world, man can be an intermediary or a mediator between God and the remainder of God's creation. Created in the image of God, man stands where the world of matter meets the world of spirit. He stands on the horizon between time and eternity, with the capability of speaking for eternity to time. He is a synthesis of the finite and the infinite. Belonging to the infinite as well as the finite, man dominates the very world that dwarfs him. The universe may crush him, but he is greater than that universe because he knows when he is being crushed.

So far we have been considering, in the main, man in his original created state. But all men have sinned and come short of the glory of God. Pascal speaks of the grandeur of man but also of his misery. Man's grandeur is the fact that he was created in the image or likeness of God; his misery is that through sin that image has been marred or defaced. But even the misery of fallen man reflects, to some degree, his grandeur or greatness. At least man knows that he is miserable. It may be miserable to know one's wickedness, but it is great to know that one is miserable. Pascal suggests that no one is unhappy at not being a king except a deposed king. Man's miseries are the miseries of a dethroned monarch. The dethroned monarch is the image of God.

Does the preceding mean that the image of God has been completely lost or destroyed? Quite evidently the answer is no. At least man retains the potential for communication with God. There is enough of the image left to serve as an "antenna of the soul," as an awareness of "a paradise lost." It serves as a point of contact for the gospel message. Otherwise our preaching and witnessing would be in vain.

The potential for fellowship with God, which even sinful man retains, largely explains the eternal restlessness of man. At the center of mans' being, there is a dialectical tension. He was created in the image of God, and yet he is a slave of sin. Sin has not only separated him from God but also from the depths of his own being. There is disunity within him rather than unity. Nevertheless, he longs for unity within himself and with God. He has an insatiable thirst for the Eternal. Whether he is aware of it or not, man is homesick for God.

If the image or likeness of God has not been destroyed, what has happened to it? It has been marred, defaced, or to use an expression of Calvin, it has been "fearfully deformed." In other words, man's true essence, which stems from or can be identified with the image of God, has been corrupted but not destroyed.

This marred or defaced image can be and is restored when man is brought into union with Christ who is "the likeness of God" (2 Cor. 4:4), "the image of the invisible God" (Col. 1:15), and who "bears the very stamp" or the

"flawless expression" (Ph.) of the nature of God (Heb. 1:3).
He is the exact reproduction of the Father. He himself said,
"He who has seen me has seen the Father" (John 14:9). The
restored image becomes a reality or is actualized in our lives
as we live in fellowship with the one who fully embodies
that image.

The restoration of the image of God through our union
with the One who is the full or complete image of the Father
establishes right relations with God, with one's self, and
with others. It unites or unifies that which has been frag-
mented or separated. But the restoration of the image also
gives us a deepened insight into the meaning and significance of the image. This, in turn, results in a clearer understanding of sin and a deepened consciousness of sin in our
lives. It seems that the more the image has been restored in
one's life, the more aware he is of his failure to realize fully
the image of God in his life.

The preceding means that the restoration of the image is
never complete. We "are being changed into his likeness
from one degree of glory to another" (2 Cor. 3:18). We
"have put on the new nature, which is being renewed in
knowledge after the image of its creator" (Col. 3:10). We
have been changed, but we are also in the process of being
changed. The image of God has been restored, but it is also
in the process of being restored. As Kierkegaard suggests,
man can only be *"on the way,"* but he must continually be
in the process of "becoming." To use a Bultmann concept,
the Christian life is always an intention and a quest.

Dignity and Worth

The companion facts that man was created in the image
of God and that Christ died to restore that image give to
man his worth and dignity, a conception that is an underly-
ing assumption of both Testaments. And let us never forget

that worth and dignity belong to man as such: to men and women, black and white, old and young, rich and poor, clean and dirty, educated and uneducated, wise and foolish, moral and immoral. No man has gone so high or so low that he has not been created in the image of God and that Christ has not died for him.

As implied, the high value placed on man is not inherent in man except as he is related to God. Separate him from God, and he belongs to the natural order or the animal world. Man is of infinite value only because he has been created in the image of God, the Infinite Person. And, incidentally, the incarnation, a part of the process to restore the image of God in man, lifted the dignity of man to its highest level.

The dignity and worth of man mean, among other things, that no man, group of men, nation, or social institution should ever manipulate or use man as a mere means. He should always be treated as an end of infinite value. This should be just as true of one man as of another, of black as well as white, of poor as well as rich.

It is doubtful if there is any concept more central in our Western way of life than the high value placed on the individual person. But let us repeat that this high value of man is derived from his actual or potential relation to God. Divorce man from God and you separate him from his source of value. Sooner or later he will lose respect not only for his fellowman but also for himself. This is the source of much of "man's inhumanity to man."

God himself respects the human person. He has created man in his own image; he will not violate that image. One aspect or expression of that image is the freedom of man. Someone has asked if God did not tremble when he created man with the freedom to say "yes" and "no" even to his Creator. Man has been called "the risk of God." But God had to take that risk if man was to be man. God wants man to cooperate with him in his work in the world but the cooperation must be voluntary. He will not override or force the will of man even to restore the marred or deformed image. Man must freely repent of his sins and open his heart to the resurrected Christ.

There is a glorious companion fact to the idea that God never treats man as a mere means. That fact or truth is that man may voluntarily make himself available to God to be used by him as a means to extend his rule, reign, or kingdom in the world. Our Christian faith places a high value on the individual person, but when properly understood it places as great if not a greater premium upon self-denial and self-sacrifice for the sake of others and particularly for the sake of the purposes of God. This idea is an integral phase of the Christian conception of individualism. The wonderful thing about it is that man finds his greatest freedom and his most complete fulfillment as he voluntarily gives himself in service to God and man. There is no greater or more central truth in the teachings of Jesus than the fact that one finds life by losing it for his sake (Matt. 16:25).

Equality and Inequality

The first sentence of the second paragraph of the Declaration of Independence is as follows: "We hold these truths to be self-evident, that all men are created equal; that they are endowed by their Creator with certain unalienable rights; that among these are life, liberty, and the pursuit of happiness." But is it self-evident that all men are created equal? The answer to this question is tremendously important for human relations and in a particular way for those relations in the contemporary world.

It seems relatively clear that men are both equal and unequal. Their equality and their inequality are both grounded in the creative work of God. Their equality stems from the fact that they are all created in the image of God. There is equality of dignity and rights accompanied by diversity or inequality of functions. The equality of men is a constant, their inequality a variant.

There are various ways in which men are not equal. They are not equal in physical strength and stamina, in mental capacity and alertness, in moral stability and character, or in spiritual discernment and sensitivity. No two human beings are exactly alike. Even identical twins are not completely identical. The fact that no two finger prints are alike is symbolic of the fact that men are characterized by variety instead of uniformity. There are many factors that contribute, to varying degrees, to this diversity or uniqueness. Among these are heredity, environment, sex, race, nationality, and temperament.

Although there is uniqueness and inequality among men, the equality of all is more significant for Christian living. Equality and equal rights are primary; differences and inequalities may be important but they are secondary. Whatever may be the differences in abilities and in functions of men, they are equal in all that is essential in being a man.

A Cadillac, a Dodge, a Ford, and a Volkswagen may differ considerably in their appearance and the way they function, but they have common characteristics that make all of them identifiable as automobiles. So it is with men. And from the Christian perspective being a man is such an important thing that differences between men, even their inequalities, are insignificant in comparison.

All men belong to one human family. They are one by creation. This does not mean sameness. Under God there is unity in diversity. There is one human race composed of many races. The Christian community includes a wide variety of persons from diverse races and cultures. They are, however, one community. All of us within the community

stand before God on the common ground of our creatureli-
ness and of our redemption through union with Christ. We
are one in creation and in re-creation.

Men are equal before God because God is equally the
God of all; Jew and Gentile, male and female, American
and Russian, employee and employer, black and white.
Those in the spiritual family of God are all equally children
of his. He is concerned about all and shares his love with
all. A deep and an abiding sense of their equality before
God is the only solid hope for equality of men before their
fellowmen.

The concept of the equality of men is very prominent in
the Scriptures, but particularly in the New Testament. Jesus, who came to reveal the Father, proved over and over
again that he was impartial or no respecter of persons. The
"no partiality" lesson was a difficult one for his disciples to
learn, even as it remains a difficult lesson for many of us
in the contemporary period. It was only after prejudiced
Peter had had a vision on a housetop and had had some
convincing conversation in the house of Cornelius that he
was ready to say, "Truly I perceive ["I see quite plainly,"
Moffatt] that God shows no partiality" (Acts 10:34). Paul
stated specifically or implied the "no partiality" principle
in many places (see Rom. 10:12; 1 Cor. 12:13; Gal. 2:6;
Col. 3:11). His statement in Galatians 3:28 is particularly
pointed: "There is no room for Jew or Greek, no room for
slave or freeman, no room for male or female, for you are
all one through union with Christ Jesus" (Wm.). Notice the
words "there is no room," which is a simple statement of
fact.

James applies the "no partiality" or "no-respecter-of-
persons" principle in a very pointed way to the church (see
2:1–9). The immediate application is to the treatment of the
rich and poor but the general principle, which is stated
twice (vv. 1, 9), would apply to any human distinctions
based on sex, age, culture, or color. And the principle ap-

plies not only to the church as the body of Christ but also to members of the body. We not only stand before God as equals, we also stand before one another as equals.

The equality principle is not only important in the church but also in political structures. There should be equality not only in the presence of God but also in the presence of Caesar. This will be true if Casesar recognizes that he stands before God with those who stand before him.

Relation to the Community

There is validity in Kierkegaard's idea of the "solitary individual," standing apart from the crowd in the sanctuary of his own soul, face to face with the Eternal. But man does not always stand alone in the presence of the Eternal. Many times he stands there in the company of others. Even when he withdraws to "the sanctuary of his own soul" he cannot escape the questioning voice of the Eternal: "Where is your brother?"

The preceding means, among other things, that the community is grounded in and evolves from the nature of man. The diversity of gifts and functions of men necessitates the community. Many of the needs of the individual must be met by others. For example, the husband and the wife need one another. They belong to one another, and each finds his or her fulfillment with the other in the community of the home.

Human communities evolve, however, from the nature of man in a deeper and more positive way. There can be no person without other persons, no "I" without a "Thou." Karl Barth suggests that God wills that man's being should find fulfillment in the relationship or the togetherness of I and thou. He says that God calls man "to find himself by affirming the other, to know joy by comforting the other, and self-expression by honouring the other." [1]

In other words, man finds his fulfillment as a person in

communication with other persons. The ultimate expression of this fulfillment is in his communion with God, but it also finds expression in his relation to his fellowmen in the human community and as a Christian in the Christian community. Man's need for communion or fellowship is the basis for communities of all types.

Although man as a person is dependent on the community, he also stands apart from the community. This dual truth stems from his divine-human nature. Belonging to the earthly or natural order he is dependent on the community, but belonging to the spiritual or transcendent order he is independent of the community. The highest point of reference in his life is God. It is God who speaks the final authoritative word to the one who has been created in his image.

The individual is so dependent, however, on the community that unbridled individualism is destructive of the best interest of the individual and the community. Both the person and the community of persons are necessary for human existence. Neither should be considered merely instrumental. Each functions for and finds fulfillment in the other. Each has both rights and responsibilities. This is true of all the communities to which the individual may belong: the play or work group, the family, the church, the neighborhood, the nation, and the world. And it should be remembered that the rights of these communities do not derive exclusively from the persons who belong to them. The basic God-ordained communities have some inherent rights as well as responsibilities.

There are limitations, however, of the rights of the group or community just as there are limitations of the rights of the individual. The groups to which the individual belongs, such as the family, the church, and particularly the state, derive a part of their authority from the consent of the people. God has seen fit to mediate a portion of his authority over the community through the people whom the community serves. Furthermore, God has reserved for himself the final word with the individual, whether as a member of a family, a church, or a citizen of the state. It is the fact that man is directly responsible to God that gives him an independence that transcends any and all communities. As one who maintains human relations, he may be under the authority of the state but as a person before God, it is the authority of God that is final in his life. The word of man and particularly the Christian is, "We must obey God rather than men" (Acts 5:39) whether as individual men or as a community of men.

The primary consideration of the Christian in his relation to the church or the Christian community is not the church's authority over him but his voluntary commitment to the church and its fellowship. When one is brought into union with Christ, he comes into the family of God. This means, among other things, that he not only commits himself to God but also to the family of God and to the members of that family. The Christian community or family is, or is supposed to be, a closely knit fellowship, characterized by a mutual love of the members for one another. This love should be so closely akin to divine love or *agape* that the members of the family would share with one another in times of need. This is the abiding lesson from the experience of the Jerusalem church as recorded in Acts. The individuals in the fellowship who had possessions sold them and brought the proceeds to the Apostles that distribution might be made to those in need.

Responsibility and Freedom

Man not only has some responsibilities to and within the Christian community; he also has some responsibilities to other human communities. The more mature he is morally and spiritually, the more conscious he will be of the rights of others and of his own responsibilities. What happened to man's sense of responsibility when he sinned and the image of God was marred, defaced, or deformed? There is still enough of the image left to make man responsible and to leave him with a sense of responsibility. He is responsible because he is still free, although admittedly his freedom is limited. He is free enough, however, to be morally responsible.

The preceding does not mean that man is exempt from the operation of the laws of heredity or the influence of environmental factors that touch his life. His home, his church, his community determine to a considerable degree what he considers to be wise or unwise, good or bad, right or wrong. But at the time of decision his will is not forced. In the final analysis what he does is determined from within. Regardless of the factors that have touched and influenced his life, man is responsible at least for the way he responds to those factors.

God who created man a person respects the freedom he gave to man, but he also holds man accountable for what he does with his freedom. Freedom is not primarily a right but a duty of man before God. Also, man's freedom evolves from his relation to God. This means that when man asserts his independence of God, he loses his real freedom. He uses his freedom to lose his freedom and to become a slave of sin. In other words, man's truest and fullest freedom is found in relationship with and in obedience to God. It is an illusion for man to believe that he can be free apart from God. Rather, we are free in God and within his will. If the Son make us free, we are free indeed (John 8:36).

The latter freedom is a freedom from the condemnation of the law but also a freedom from the enslavement of sin. This freedom belongs only to the redeemed child of God, and regretfully we must admit only potentially and progressively to him. In reality he remains enslaved to sin, but in his union with Christ there begins in his life a movement away from sin and hence an increasing freedom from the enslavement of sin. One reason for the movement away from sin is a keener sensitivity to sin and a deeper sense of responsibility for sin. Furthermore, the maturing child of God recongizes that just as his redemption is of grace so his increasing freedom from the enslavement of sin is also a work of grace. The coonsciousness that all is of grace places the Christian under an abiding obligation to live a life worthy of that grace. Here is the soundest possible basis for everyday Christian living. Grace and goodness belong together. Ours is a "therefore" morality or ethic.

FOR THOUGHT AND DISCUSSION

1. How is the fact that man is created in the image of God related to such diverse problems as sex relations before, within, and outside of marriage, common-law marriages, euthanasia, and relations with other classes and colors?

2. What is your viewpoint concerning capital punishment? Is there anything in this chapter that you can use to defend your position? Some people contend that it is taught in the Scriptures. To what scriptures do they usually refer—Old Testament or New Testament? Would those who defend capital punishment on the basis of the Old Testament justify its use for all of the causes or offenses indicated in the Old Testament (ten to twelve)?

3. Among the many positions or perspectives concerning abortion there are the following rather well-defined views:

    (1) The decision about an abortion should be left entirely to the woman and her doctor.

    (2) A suggested model law, enacted by some state

legislatures, would permit abortions for the following reasons:

(a)   where the physical, mental, or emotional health of the woman would be endangered

(b)   where there is a good chance that the child would be born with serious physical and/or mental abnormalities

(c)   in the case of rape or incest.

(3)   Permitted only when the continuance of the pregnancy would endanger the life of the mother.

(4)   No abortion under any conditions.

Assuming that any legalized abortion would be performed by a licensed physician and in a registered hospital, which, if any, of the preceding most closely represents your position? How would you defend your position? How is it related to the material in this chapter?

IV
The Biblical Revelation

The Christian interpretation of the nature of God and the nature of man, discussed in the preceding chapters, is heavily indebted to the Scriptures. Most of the content of those chapters was based upon and was an interpretation of biblical material. The Bible provides, however, a foundation in more direct ways for an emphasis on everyday Christian living. In contrast to the subjective or inner motivation that evolves from the Christian's experience in and with the resurrected Christ, the Bible serves as an objective source of motivation for the Christian life. It also contains concepts and principles that can provide guidelines for the child of God in times of decision.

Its Nature

The Bible, a book of many books, "a library of Hebrew literature," a religious anthology, is in a unique sense a divine-human book. Its twofold nature can be summed up by saying that the Bible is the record of the revelation from God, of God, through men, to men.

This dual nature of the Bible is clearly evident in the process of its writing. The initiative for or the origin of the revelation which gave birth to the Bible was from God. God has sought through the centuries to reveal himself to all men. He has done this through nature, history, and providence. This is called general revelation in contrast to the special revelation recorded in the Scriptures. Self-disclosure is even necessary, to some degree, for one to have a knowledge of the inner life and character of a human person. This becomes infinitely more true of any knowledge that we may be able to comprehend of the divine Person. He must initiate the process and constantly work in and through the process if we are to comprehend the revelation.

The revelation that produced the Bible was initiated by God and it was mediated to and through men. Hence, in a sense, the Bible is the product of man's understanding and interpretation of God's revelation and manifestation of himself. There would be no Bible without the revelation of God and no Bible without the response of men to that revelation. In other words, to use an idea of Emil Brunner, revelation is a transitive event. A transitive verb has a subject but also an object. God is the subject of the revelation; man is the object or recipient.

The twofold nature of the Bible is recognized in the Bible itself. Jesus said, "David himself, inspired by the Holy Spirit, declared. . ." (Mark 12:36). Peter similarly said: "The Holy Spirit spoke beforehand by the mouth of David. . ." (Acts 1:16). The Holy Spirit did the speaking, but he used the mouth of David. There are frequent references to the Mosaic authorship of portions of the Old Testament.[1]

The relation of the divine to the human in the writing of the Bible is rather clearly stated in 2 Peter 1:21: "No prophecy ever came by the impulse of man ("from the will of men," TEV), but men moved ("carried along, " TEV) by the Holy Spirit spoke from God." Men did the speaking, but they spoke "from God" and we might add primarily "for" or "concerning" God. Since finite men were the instruments to whom and through whom God spoke, the revelation, which might be considered a constant, varied with the individuals who received it. It was inevitably colored some by their personalities.

We should not forget, however, that through all the human processes of the Bible there is a divine process. In that divine process man comes face to face with God. It is this confrontation that changes the "historic word" into the "living Word." This is true of us as we come face to face with God in the revelation or self-disclosure that we find recorded in the Scriptures. It then becomes for us *The Word of God*. It becomes a living, dynamic reality in our lives. The word has the capacity to become the living Word because it was originally living word when God revealed himself to his spokesmen.

The Bible is not only the divine-human book in its authorship but also in its content. We not only find in the Bible a record of God's revelation concerning his nature and character. We also find revealed God's attitude toward, relation to, and will for man. Furthermore, the Scriptures not only record the movement of God among men, they also portray the life struggles, the faults and failures, as well as the successes of real men and women. This is another factor that helps to explain the continuing popularity of the Bible. Men and women through the centuries have seen so much of themselves in the characters of the Bible. Or, on the other hand, they have seen in the lives of some of God's saints qualities that have challenged them and lifted them to higher levels of living.

Another very evident characteristic of the Bible is its unity in the midst of its diversity. This fact stems from its divine-human nature. Its unity is derived primarily from its divine nature while its diversity stems from its human nature.

Diversity in content, in emphasis, in general approach and style, and even in moral tone is rather obvious. This was more or less inevitable since God had to use finite, sinful men as the recipients of or channels for his self-disclosure. They were limited in their capacity to interpret that revelation and to some degree even to receive it. This limitation was inevitable unless God was to use those men as inanimate objects completely under his dominance and control. The latter could not be true if men were to continue to be men and if God was to continue to be the kind of God we find revealed in the Scriptures. It is also to be remembered that some of the diversity stems from the fact that the people in general were unprepared to accept the full revelation of God. This is the background for the statement of Jesus that Moses permitted them to divorce their wives because of their "hardness of heart." In other words, the limitation was not on the part of Moses but on the part of the people.

The diversity found in the Bible means that the unity that we find there is not a static unity, but to use a recurring expression of H. H. Rowley, it is "a dynamic unity" or a "unity of growth." [2] The developmental nature of this unity is clear within the Old Testament. It is particularly recognizable when one moves from the Old Testament into the New Testament.

The "unity of growth" or the "dynamic unity" so evident in the Bible stems from the central dynamic event that the Bible records and on which it reflects. That event was the life, the death, and the resurrection of Christ. The Old Testament looks forward to that event; the Gospels, in the main, record it, while the remainder of the New Testament reflects it. That event threads all the parts of the Bible, Old Testament and New Testament, on one string. It gives a unity to the Bible that in some ways is its most striking feature.

Another way of saying the same thing is to say that what makes the two Testaments a real unity is the fact that the New Testament proclaims present what the Old Testament points to as future. The former is a confirmation and crowning of the latter. It was Jesus himself who said, "You search the scriptures, because you think that in them you have eternal life; and it is they that bear witness to me"

(John 5:39). The Scriptures bear witness. They point beyond themselves. Any passage is best understood when we consider where it points rather than what it specifically says. The revelation may be given "in many and various ways" (Heb. 1:1), but it always points to the same Person and to the same purpose, which is the redemption of man. It is this, a divine Person with a consistent purpose, that explains the unity of the Bible.

As an evidence and expression of this basic unity grounded in the divine Person, there are some unifying concepts or motifs that are more or less prevalent in both Testaments. One of those, mentioned previously, is the kinship appeal or the expectation that the children of God will be like him. Another important concept or motif is the covenant, prevalent in both Testaments. God is revealed in the Scriptures as the initiator of the covenant. He establishes the conditions of the covenant, and his people accept those conditions. When we move into the New Testament, the church becomes the covenant community. There is also a sense in which the individual Christian has entered into covenant with God and also with the people of God.

Its Climax

The revelation of God recorded in the Bible, a divine-human book, is climaxed in Christ, a divine-human Person We find in him the climax of the self-disclosure of God. God's final and perfect word concerning his own nature and character is found in Christ: in his life, his death, his resurrection. Notice the words "in Christ." The climax of the revelation is not "through Christ" but "in Christ." Jesus himself said, "He who has seen me has seen the Father" (John 14:9, cf. 17:22). Again he said, "I and the Father are one" (John 10:30). In him "the full nature of God chose to live" (Col. 1:19, Ph.). Also, in him God gave "a full and complete expression of Himself" (Col. 2:9, Ph.). Or, as the writer of Hebrews says, Christ bore "the very stamp" or "the perfect representation" (Wm.) of God's nature. Christ is "God focused."

Christ is also the climax of God's revelation of his attitude toward and will for man. This revelation is most fully and clearly revealed in what Christ was, in the quality or kind of life he lived. It is also revealed through the things he taught. He himself, in the comparisons that he made between the Law and the interpretation of the Law and the principles of his Kingdom, said, "You have heard that it was said. . . But I say to you. . ." (Matt.5:21, 27, 33, 38, 43). What he said was final and authoritative. In response to the pressing question of the Pharisees concerning divorce he replied, "For your hardness of heart Moses allowed you to divorce your wives, but from the beginning it was not so, and I say to you. . ." (Matt. 19:8-9). Notice "from the beginning" and "I say to you." What he said was in harmony with God's original purpose, and we might add with God's ultimate plan or will. Notice as suggested previously that the imperfections of the Law regarding divorce were attributed to the people rather than to Moses. This suggests that even God is limited by the immaturity and spiritual insensitivity of those to whom he wants to speak. This is one reason why the incarnation was necesary for the supreme or complete revelation of God.

The recognition of Christ as the final and full revelation of the Father tends to make Christianity in the strictest sense not a religion of a book but a religion of a Person. The book itself is reverenced primarily because of the Person whose life, ministry, death, and resurrection are recorded there. It is he who is the Way, the Truth, the Resurrection, the Bread of Life, and the Light of the World. Christ is God's final and full word to man. It is a word that not only reveals God to man but simultaneously it reveals man to himself. We see in Christ, the God-man, what God is like and what man, by the grace of God, should become.

The fact that the revelation of God is climaxed in Christ means that there is movement from promise to fulfillment, from the Old Testament to the New Testament. This means that the Old Testament should always be interpreted and particularly evaluated in the light of the fuller revelation in the New Testament. This is true although the basic concepts of both the Old Testament and New Testament "are intrinsically and historically inseparable." [3]

The preceding does not mean that the Old Testament is not a legitimate part of the Christian Bible. It forms a unity with the New Testament, but it is a unity of growth or progress. The unity is dynamic, not static. This means, among other things, that the ethical teachings of the Bible are not on a plain; they represent a part of a path. While the path does not always move smoothly, the over-all movement is upward. Rowley likens the two Testaments to the germ (Old) and the fruit (New). He also compares the relation of the Testaments to the parts of a musical sonata. For example, he says that the New Testament is the final climactic movement but that the Old Testament belongs as a part of the sonata. As G. Ernest Wright suggests, although the Old Testament is incomplete, yet the New Testament no more than the Old Testament can stand alone. It is a completion and fulfillment of the Old.[4] Sometimes the movement is simply one of emphasis. For example, the emphasis in the New Testament is more on principle, less on law, more inner less outer, more positive less negative.

There is a sense in which the revelation of God continues to be progressive. At least that is true of our comprehension, understanding, and application of it to life situations.

Its Content

Broadly speaking, the Bible contains a twofold message:
(1) how men can be saved, and (2) how saved men are to
live. The latter involves more than one dimension of life. To
use an expression of Bonhoeffer, when one becomes a child
of God, he is plunged "into many different dimensions of
life simultaneously." Life for him becomes "multi-dimen-
sional and polyphonous." [5] These "many different dimensions," however, can be compressed in the main into two
major emphases or dimensions. How saved men are to live
(1) in relation to God (the vertical), and (2) in relation to
their fellowmen (the horizontal). The horizontal dimension
not only involves one's relation to his fellowmen as individuals; it also includes his relation to society and to the various groups and organizations to which he may belong or
with which he may maintain some contact.

While the Bible clearly reveals that right relations to God
and man belong together, it is also clear that right relations
to God are most basic. This is another evidence that God
and not man is central in the biblical perspective. When
stated together, right relations to God are stated first followed by right relations to one's fellowman. The latter is in
a sense a derivative of the former, but it is an inevitable
derivative. It is so natural and inevitable that if one is not
right in his relations to his fellowman that fact is a valid
reason to conclude that he is not right with God.

The fact that right relations to God are basic but that
right relations to one's fellowman naturally follows is illus-
trated over and over again in the Scriptures. For example,
the first of the Ten Commandments relate to man's relation
to God; later ones refer to his relation to his fellowman.
When Jesus was asked, "Which is the great commandment
in the law" his answer was, "You shall love the Lord your
God with all your heart, and with all your soul, and with

all your mind." He then said, "This is the great and first commandment," and possibly after a pause for emphasis, he added, "And a second is like it, you shall love your neighbor as yourself" (Matt. 22:36–39; see Deut. 6:5 and Lev. 19:18). Like the first, it is a commandment of love but possibly it is also like it in importance. The two belong together. They are the fulfillment of the law and the prophets (Matt. 22:40, Rom. 13:8–10, Gal. 5:14). Furthermore, the love of our fellowman is the proof of our love for God (1 John 3:14–15; 4:7–8, 16, 17, 20–21).

The relation of faith and works is additional evidence of the close inter-relatedness of right relations to God and to man. It is abundantly clear that salvation comes by faith alone apart from works, but the purpose of that salvation is good works or a life of goodness (Eph. 2:8–10; cf. Matt. 5:14–16, John 15:16). The proof of the faith that saves is the quality of life that is lived (Matt. 7:15–23, Rom. 6:1–4, 1 John 2:3–6, James 2:14–26). Jesus also plainly stated that one cannot have the forgiveness of God unless he forgives those who have sinned against him (Matt. 6:12–15; 18:21–35). Only the forgiving heart can be forgiven.

This two-dimensional emphasis, right relation to God and man, is more or less evident throughout the Bible. It is implied if not specifically stated in the great "therefore" passages in the Old Testament as well as in the New Testament. In the former, "therefore" usually represents a transition from a description of the sins of the people to the judgment of God. In the New Testament "therefore" frequently introduces exhortations to Christian living based on the mercies or grace of God (e.g., Rom. 12:1; Eph. 4:1). The latter is what makes Christian morality "therefore morality." Goodness, whatever the Christian may have or practice, is based on or is a result of the grace of God.

The word 'therefore" usually ties together what in reality is inseparable or indivisible. In many and possibly in most cases, if the "therefore" were omitted, one-half of the statement would be an irrelevant statement about God while the other half would be an impossible expectation or demand of man. This is particularly true of the "therefore" passages in the New Testament.

Since right relations to God and man are so closely interrelated, it is natural that the reverse would also be true: a man cannot be wrong in relation to God or man without being wrong with the other. This is stated with unusual clarity concerning one's being wrong with his fellowman. Such a man cannot be right with God. For example, sin against one's fellowman is really and finally sin against God. This may be the explanation for David's statement to Nathan, "I have sinned against the Lord" (2 Sam. 12:13). He later cried out:

> Against thee, thee only, have I sinned,
>   and done that which is evil in thy sight (Ps. 51:4).

Does this mean that David had not sinned against Uriah and his family? Certainly not. Sin is bidirectional. It is sin against God and man but against man in God. At least man is in God in the sense that he has been created in the image of God, which gives to him value in the sight of God. Any sin against man is really sin against God and ultimately against not only the command of God but also against the nature of God. Here is the real and final basis for the close relation of morality and religion or right relation to God and man in the Bible.

The twofold emphasis on right relation to God and man is at least implied in the statement that the boy Jesus increased "in favor with God and man" (Luke 2:52). The instruction from the apostles concerning the qualifications for the seven suggested that they were to "men of good repute, full of the Holy Spirit and wisdom" (Acts 6:3). Paul suggested that bishops were to be "well thought of by outsiders" (1 Tim. 3:7), while Peter suggested that Christians should "maintain good conduct among the Gentiles" (1 Pet. 2:12).

The cross symbolizes the two-dimensional relations of the Christian life. The upright bar represents the vertical, man reaching up to God. The cross rests on the good earth, which is identified as God's creation. The transverse beam symbolizes man reaching out to other men and to the society of men.

Its Relevance

The relevance of the Bible stems basically from the Person revealed there. He is the eternal "I AM," the same yesterday, today, and forevermore. His self-disclosure or self-manifestation which gave birth to the Bible is abidingly relevant to men since men were created for fellowship with him.

The redemptive message of the Bible, which is God's good news to men, is also continuously relevant. Men of the contemporary age and of every age need its message of salvation. Also, the great promises of the Scriptures are just as relevant and meaningful today as in generations past. Some of the better known of these are: "The eternal God is thy refuge, and underneath are the everlasting arms" (Deut. 33.27, KJV); "The Lord is my shepherd; I shall not want" (Ps. 23:1, KJV); "Come to me, all who labor and are heavy-laden, and I will give you rest" (Matt. 11:28); "And we know that in everything God works for good with those who love him, who are called according to his purpose" (Rom. 8:28).

What about the moral or ethical teachings of the Bible? Are these relevant for us in our day? Our primary interest in this study is in the day-by-day responsibilities and relationships of the Christian life. Can the contemporary Christian find in the Bible material that will be relevant and helpful to him in his daily decisions? We believe he can and will if he has the proper perspective concerning the Christian life and concerning the Bible.

Regarding the Bible, let us suggest that the Bible is not a rule book to which one can turn for a chapter and verse answer for every question or a solution for every problem. While the basic needs of men remain relatively the same from age to age, their specific problems vary a great deal. This means, among other things, that the Bible contains the answers to man's basic needs but it does not contain specific answers for many of his problems. Really, some of his problems were unknown in biblical times.

There are also portions of the Bible that were so thoroughly historically conditioned that they do not apply to our day. They were written to meet the needs of a particular group of people faced with particular problems at a particular point in time. An example is the ceremonial laws of the Old Testament. We do not consider them applicable to or relevant for us in our day except in indirect and tangential ways. The same is true of some things found in the New Testamant, particularly in the Pauline epistles. The latter were written, in the main, to particular groups with some distinctive problems. If Paul was to meet their needs, he had to direct his remarks and instructions pointedly and specifically to those needs. One such need or problem that Paul discussed in more than one epistle was the eating of meat offered to idols. (Rom. 14 and 1 Cor. 8; cf. Acts 15:29).

A careful examination, however, of some of the so-called irrelevant portions of the Bible will reveal principles that are abidingly relevant. The latter is seen with particular clarity concerning the eating of meat offered to idols. There are evident at least two principles that apply just as much today as then. They are as follows: (1) Right for a child of

God is not decided exclusively by what he considers right but also by what others consider right for him. (2) An activity that may be right within itself can become positively wrong or sinful because of its effect on others.

The preceding correctly implies that the most relevant portions of the Bible are its principles or ideals. And contrary to the view of many, the most constantly relevant portions are its ideals of perfection. These ideals, which Reinhold Niebuhr once labeled "impossible possibilities," will challenge us to the end of life's journey, standing in constant judgment upon our very imperfect approximation of the ideals. They are above and beyond history, eternally transcendent but also, and for that reason, eternally relevant. These ideals of perfection create the dynamic tension at the heart of our Christian faith, which, in turn, is the secret to its creativity.

FOR THOUGHT AND DISCUSSION

1. What are some of the problems created for those who accept the Old Testament as equally authoritative with the New Testament? Consider problems such as capital punishment, mentioned in the last chapter, war, God's relation to war, relation of races, and legalism in general. Does the statement of Jesus, "You have heard that it was said to the men of old. . .but I say to you" (Matt. 5:21, 27, 31, 33, 38, 43) and what he said concerning divorce, "Moses allowed you. . .and I say to you" (Matt. 19:8, 9) help us to evaluate properly the Old Testament as an authoritative word from God? Must it always be evaluated in the light of the full revelation in Christ?

2. If you can think of God using the writers of the Scriptures somewhat like a business or professional man

uses a secretary, which of the following would most accurately describe your conception of the way he used them:

(1)   Dictated punctuation and the spelling of difficult or unusual words as well as the paragraphing.

(2)   Indicated paragraphing only, trusting the writers with spelling and punctuation.

(3)   Gave the writers the general content of what he wanted to say and trusted them with the writing. Checked to see that the basic content was accurate.

3.   Jesus said that the Sabbath was made for man and not man for the Sabbath. Could the same be said for every basic moral law or expectation of God? In other words, are the laws and commands of God in harmony with our natures and provided for our good? Can you see the relation of your answer to this question to commandments such as "You shall not commit adultery"? Can you see the relation of all of the preceding to John's statement, "and his commandments are not burdensome" (1 John 5:3)?

V

The Christian Experience

Three foundations of or sources for an emphasis on everyday Christian living have been discussed: the nature of God, the nature of man, and the nature of the biblical revelation. In this chapter we shall consider another source for such an emphasis: the nature of the Christian's experience in and with Christ.

When this experience is properly interpreted, it leads naturally to an emphasis on everyday Christian living. The Christian life is not primarily a theory about life but rather it is a way of life, and a distinct way. From another viewpoint, we can correctly say that Christian living is not an external attachment to the Christian's life; rather, it evolves from the nature of his life in Christ. The outer expressions of that life are the results of an inner relationship of the child of God with the resurrected Christ.

The Initial Experience

There can be no question about man's need for some experience that will basically change the perspective and direction of his life. Our experience as well as the Bible has taught us that "all we like sheep have gone astray" (Isa. 53:6), that "none is righteous, no, not one" (Rom. 3:10), that "all have sinned and fall short of the glory of God" (Rom. 3:23). Man needs help from outside himself to overcome sin in his life. He receives that help when he comes into union with the resurrected Christ.

There are different terms in the New Testament that are

used to express the idea of the Christian's union with Christ. One of the most familiar and most meaningful of those expressions is "in Christ," a favorite of Paul. Deissmann says that these or comparable words such as "in Christ Jesus," "in the Lord," "in him" occur 164 times in Paul's epistles.[1] The words or "formula" are somewhat comparable in their uniqueness in Paul's epistles to his well-known trilogy of faith, hope, and love. Outside of Paul's epistles "in Christ" is found in the New Testament only once in Hebrews (3:14) and three times in First Peter (3:16; 5:10, 14).

A glance at a few of the many occurrences of "in Christ" in Paul's epistles will reveal something of the richness of the life the child of God has or can have in his union with Christ. Paul says that our redemption. . ."is in Christ Jesus" (Rom. 3:24), that we are made "alive to God in Jesus" (Rom. 6:11), and to the Galatians he wrote, "In Christ Jesus you are all sons of God through faith" (Gal. 3:26). In addition, the freedom that we have as Christians is in Christ Jesus (Gal. 2:24). We are sanctified in him (1 Cor. 1:2), are one body in him (Rom. 12:5), are "fellow workers in Christ Jesus" (Rom. 16:3), are all one in him (Gal. 3:28), and have been made to sit "in heavenly places in Christ Jesus" (Eph. 2:6). Paul also speaks of the "upward call of God in Christ Jesus" (Phil. 3:14), a call that will create a continuous tug in our lives. In the great chapter on the resurrection Paul speaks of those who have "fallen asleep in Christ" (1 Cor. 15:18). We should be grateful that those who are "in Christ shall all be made alive" (1 Cor. 15:22) and "so we shall always be with the Lord" (1 Thess. 4:17). We are in Christ; Christ is in us. This union is so vital that it can be compared to the air we breathe. We are in the air, and the air is in us.

The idea of union with Christ is not restricted in the Pauline writings to the formula or words "in Christ." There are places where "through Christ" is used in a way strikingly similar to "in Christ" (see 2 Cor. 3:4, 14). Furthermore, to the Romans Paul said, "You are called to belong to Jesus Christ" (Rom. 1:6) and exhorted them to "put on the Lord Jesus Christ" (Rom 13:14). To the strife-torn Corinthians he said, "You are Christ's; and Christ is God's" (1 Cor. 3:23). He also said that their bodies were members of Christ (1 Cor. 6:15) and that they formed or belonged to the body of Christ: "we were all baptized into one body" (1 Cor. 12:13; cf. Rom. 6:3), we "are the body of Christ and individually members of it" (1 Cor. 12:27). Applying other words of Paul to our own lives we can say that Christ in us is our hope of glory (Col. 1:27), that we have been raised with Christ (Col. 3:1), that our lives are hid with Christ in God (Col. 3:3)—hid in the sense of both concealment and safety. Also, as we have received "Christ Jesus the Lord," we should "so live in him" (Col. 2:6). Paul also uses the term "with Christ" (see Rom. 8:32; 2 Cor. 13:4; Phil. 1:2; 2 Thess. 4:17; 5:10).

In two places where Paul pictures as fully as anywhere his own close personal relationship to the resurrected Christ, he does not use the words "in Christ." For example, he says, "It is no longer I who live, but Christ who lives in me" (Gal. 2:20) and again, "For to me to live is Christ, and to die is gain" (Phil. 1:21).

Two things are necessary for one to have the experience which brings him into union with Christ. There must be the outreach of God to man matched by the outreach or upreach of man to God. The first is grace, the second is faith. The initiative comes from God, the response from man. God is the acting power in man's salvation, man the reacting power. But he must react, he must take the leap of faith.

The Continuing Experience

Union with Christ is not only an initial experience but also a continuing and growing one. We have been made new creations in Christ Jesus. Just as surely we are in the process of being made into his likeness. In a sense we are being called to be what we already are. These two aspects of our union with Christ, the past and the present, but particularly the latter, are expressed in a distinctly Johannine word: abide or abides.[2] It is comparable in meaning to Paul's "in Christ," although Paul's term is more frequently applied to the initial Christian experience.

The word "abide" as it applies to the Christian's relation to Christ is particularly prevalent in the great Vine and Branches chapter (John 15) and in First John. In the former, Jesus revealed that he considered the union or relation of his disciples to him so close and vital that it could be compared to a vine and its branches. The branches are not separate from the vine; they are an integral part of the vine. The sap or life blood of the vine flows into and through the branches. It is the source of their life and their fruitfulness. No wonder he said, "Apart from me you can do nothing" (v. 5).

There are two places in First John where the concept of abiding in Christ is in a setting that gives them special significance for the Christian life. The first one is: "All who keep his commandments abide in him" (3:24). The other statement which should be tremendously challenging to every Christian is as follows: "Here is the test by which we can make sure that we are in him: whoever claims to be dwelling in him, binds himself to live as Christ himself lived" (2:6, NEB) or he "ought to walk in the same way in which he walked."

The preceding correctly suggests that being a Christian means primarily a commitment to and communion with the resurrected Christ. This in turn means commitment to his way of life. The test of our lives is not so much what we believe about the historic Jesus as it is our relation to the resurrected Christ. The acceptance of certain basic doctrines or dogmas is important, but more important is one's relation to the Divine Person. Doctrines or beliefs are important, but we should keep them in proper perspective. One may be rigidly orthodox in his beliefs and thoroughly unchristian in his relationships and attitudes. He may even attempt to make orthodoxy a substitute for everyday Christian living. It is easier to "believe" than to "practice."

This means that one is wrong when he considers any person a good Christian simply because of his adherence to a particular doctrine, the absence in his life of a certain vice, or the presence of a particular virtue. The good Christian is one who is so vitally related to the resurrected Christ that this relationship inevitably affects every area and relation of his life. The kind of life he lives flows so naturally from his union with Christ that he is largely unconscious of the kind and quality of life he lives. This is increasingly true as he matures in his experience with Christ.

An outgoing life of service for God and to our fellowman was the basic purpose of the initial experience when we became new creations through union with Christ. We were not saved just to be saved. There was a purpose in that initial experience that reached far beyond the experience itself. Paul suggested what he considered the normal Christian experience when he said: "For by grace you have been saved through faith; and this is not your own doing, it is the gift of God—not because of works, lest any man should boast. For we are his workmanship, created in Christ Jesus for good works" (Eph. 2:8–10). Particularly important for the Christian life is the purpose of the salvation: "for good works" or "good deeds." It was Martin Luther who said, "Our faith in Christ does not free us from works but from false opinions concerning works, that is, from the foolish presumption that justification is acquired by works."

There is a statement by Jesus in the wonderful Vine and Branches chapter that sets forth the same perspective. He said to his disciples: "You did not choose me, but I chose you and appointed you that you should go and bear fruit" (John 15:16). Notice the purpose of the choosing: "that you should go and bear fruit." He did not choose them, and he does not choose us simply to enjoy fellowship with him, as rich and rewarding as that can be. No, he chose us to bear fruit, and we bear fruit as we abide in him.

Through our union with Christ there is created within us a desire to bear fruit for him. There is also born within us new motives, a new dynamic, a new desire to know and do his will. We discover in our union with the resurrected Christ not only a new desire but also a new power to move in the direction of the purposes of God for our lives. Notice it says "to move in the direction of." We can say with Paul that we have not "already obtained," we are not "already perfect." Can we honestly also say with Paul, "But I press on to make it my own, because Christ Jesus has made me his own" (Phil. 3:12)?

There are three terms that summarize the rich blessings that come to our lives as a result of our union with and abiding in the resurrected Christ: justification, sanctification, and glorification. These are different ways of looking at our salvation in Christ. We are saved in all tenses: past, present, and future.

The Maturing Experience

Maturity in and for Christ operates in the present tense. It represents the sanctification aspect of our salvation.

The more mature the Christian, the more he realizes that his union with Christ has brought into his life a richness and fulness that he not only had not known but that he had not dreamed could be true. He discovers that the more fully he abides in Christ, the more abundant life becomes for him. He comes to understand clearly that life in Christ may mean death, but it is life in and through death. He finds that his union with Christ does not limit his life but releases new sources of life within him. Life in Christ for him does not mean the loss of freedom; rather it brings real freedom (John 8:36). It does not isolate him from people; rather it results in a more meaningful and inclusive outreach to and for people. Paul says that as he matures in Christ he will have not only a better understanding of and a changed attitude toward sin, he will also maintain a different relation to it.

The preceding and other blessings that result from our union with Christ do not come automatically and have not been fully realized in our lives. For example, there is a sense in which old things have passed away but a very real sense in which they are in the process of passing away. To use Paul's terms, we "have put on the new nature," but the new nature "is being renewed in knowledge after the image of its creator" (Col. 3:10): "have put on"—past; "being renewed"—present which reaches into the future.

Let us mention again a very meaningful paradox in the Christian life, a paradox that may be expressed in various ways. The more mature we are in Christ, the more conscious we will be that our union with him is imperfect and incomplete. Another way of expressing the same idea is to say that our union with the resurrected Christ is both the end and in a very real sense the beginning of our search for meaning in life. In him there is both release from tension and the creation of tension.

This paradox is closely related to the place of the indicative and imperative in the Christian life. As we mature in Christ, the outward expressions of the Christian life will flow more naturally from the vitality of our relation with Christ. In other words, life will be lived more and more in the indicative mood. We will do what we do not so much because we are commanded to do so but because we want to. But none of us is so mature that we do not need the imperatives of life. Really, as someone has suggested, the indicatives of the Christian life are veiled imperatives. The outer expressions of the Christian life are so much an inevitable phase of our union with Christ that if those outer expressions do not take place as indicatives they then become imperatives.

The indicative and imperative are two sides of the same coin. They maintain an inner unity. Such unity is evident in the area of love. The obligation or imperative to love one another stems from the love we have received from God. It is John who says, "Beloved, if God so loved us, we also ought to love one another" (1 John 4:11), and "We love, because he first loved us" (1 John 4:19). Lehmann, who gives primary emphasis to the indicative, suggests that there is "an imperative pressure exerted by an indicative situation." [3] Thielicke, somewhat reversing the order, suggests that the imperative is "a demand that we should attain to that starting point where the automatic process goes into operation." [4]

The preceding means, among other things, that there should be a growing or maturing experience with, in, and for Christ. We were born babes in Christ, but babies are supposed to grow. Growth is so much the nature of a babe that if he is not growing we know that something is wrong. The same is just as true of moral and spiritual babes. We were born babes but babes *in Christ*. The "in Christ" means that growth is natural, even inevitable. If growth is not evident we had better examine to see if a birth has taken place.

Unfortunately, entirely too many Christians are satisfied

to be ordinary or mediocre. It is Trueblood who says that we are plagued with a mild sort of religiosity. He also suggests that contemporary Christians are equally shocked at hearing the faith denied or seeing it practiced. Mediocre Christians, to use a distinction that Kierkegaard makes, may be admirers of Christ but not followers of him. He suggests that "a follower is or strives *to be* what he admires; an admirer holds himself personally aloof, consciously or unconsciously, he does not discern that the object of his admiration makes a claim upon him to be or to strive to be the thing he admires." [5]

The ultimate measure of our maturity in and for Christ is how much we are like him. To the little group of disciples the resurrected Christ said, "As the Father has sent me, even so I send you" (John 20:21). He was sent not to do his own will but the will of him that had sent him. We as his disciples are sent not to do our own will but his will. He was sent to be the redeemer of men; we are sent to be a redeeming influence among men. He was sent to reveal the Father; we are sent to reveal him. He was God incarnate, God in human flesh; we are to be Christ incarnate, Christ walking among men.

Paul suggested that one purpose of the work of the apostles, prophets, evangelists, pastors, and teachers was the equipment of God's people for the "building up of the body of Christ, until we all attain. . .to a mature manhood and to a perfect measure of Christ's moral stature" (Eph. 4:12–13, Wm.). How do we measure up when we stand beside the moral stature of Christ? Every one of us surely hangs his head in shame and admits that he falls far short of being what he ought to be. But what about the goal of our lives, what about the deep intentionality of our souls that motivates us and at the same time provides the measuring stick for our lives? It is possible that God judges us far more by the intent of our lives than by their achievement. Kierkegaard concludes that one is not "eternally responsible for whether he reaches his goal within this world of time. But without exception, he is eternally responsible for the kind of measure he uses." [6] He compares the reaching of the goal with hitting the mark, while the means used are comparable to taking aim. He concludes that "the aim is a more reliable indication of the marksman's goal than the spot the shot strikes." [7] The latter may be purely accidental.

In other words, the test of our lives is not so much where we are but where we are going. Have we set for ourselves a worthy goal? The most comprehensive and worthy goal for a child of God is to be like Christ. Are we progressing toward that goal? Are we more like him today than yesterday, this week than last week, this month than last month, this year than last year? It was Calvin who said, "Our labour is not lost when to-day is better than yesterday." [8]

A few additional statements need to be made concerning the methods for or means of our moral and spiritual maturing. How can we become more like Christ? How can we become a more effective channel through which he can reach out to meet the needs of people around us? We can meet, at least to some degree, certain necessary conditions for spiritual growth such as Bible reading and study, prayer and meditation, worship and fellowship in the Christian community, service in church and world, and a favorable response to what we interpret to be God's will for our lives. We can have and need to have a deepening purpose to move toward conformity to Christ.

The more mature we become, however, the more we will realize that there is comparatively little we can do consciously to become more and more conformed to the image of God in Christ. He is the one who does the "conforming" or changing. Our sanctification as well as our justification is by grace. The main thing we can do is to seek as best we can to let the resurrected Christ live in and express himself through us. If we will turn him lose in our lives, he will make us more and more into his image. This is the most effective means for our maturing in Christ. Without this, all of our conscious efforts will be in vain. It is even dangerous for us consciously to strive to make ourselves a saint. Pascal says that he who "would be an angel becomes a beast." At least there are few things more pathetic than a "self-conscious saint." In his self-consciousness he has lost whatever saintliness he possessed. The preceding means that growth or maturity in Christ is first inner but is so vitally inner that it inevitably expresses itself outwardly. Here is the real ground or foundation for everyday Christian living.

The Worship Experience

This discussion of the Christian experience as a foundation for the Christian life would not be complete without at least a brief consideration of worship. Worship is an integral part of our union with Christ. The more real and mature the latter is the more important will be the place of worship in our lives. In turn, worship is an important factor in keeping our sense of union with Christ constantly fresh and alive. Worship is essential to growth or maturity in Christ and is also expressive of that maturity.

We shall not be concerned here with a discussion of worship in general. We shall restrict our consideration to the relation of worship and service. In other words, we want to seek an answer to the question: How is worship related to everyday Christian living? And by "worship" we mean the normal response of the Christian to the consciousness of the presence of God, when the spirit of man rises to meet the Spirit of the living God. Man is awed by the sense of the Presence of God and cries out, "Here am I, send me." The natural outcome and final objective of worship is action.

Reflection might convince us that we are not as effective in our Christian lives as we should be because worship, in private as well as in the home and at the church, has not been given as prominent a place in our lives as it should have. This may be particularly true of many of us who are identified with one of the more activistic Protestant churches and/or denominations. Many individuals and churches need to heed the admonition of the resurrected Christ to his disciples: "Stay ("tarry," KJV) in the city, until you are clothed with power from on high" (Luke 24:49). Then and then only would the disciples be equipped to be his witnesses in "Jerusalem and in all Judea and Samaria and to the end of the earth" (Acts 1:8). We need to cultivate the art of tarrying until we are conscious of his presence, until we feel the touch of the divine Spirit. Our going into the world to witness for him by the spoken word and by the life we live will be effective to the degree that we have been "clothed with power from on high."

The preceding correctly suggests that worship and service are inextricably linked together. To a considerable degree, they interact on and are dependent on one another. For example, as Bonhoeffer says, "For the Christian, worship cannot be divorced from the service of the brethren. . . . If we despise our brother our worship is insincere, and forfeits every divine promise." Bonhoeffer's conclusion is: "So long as we refuse to love and serve our brother. . .whether we do so individually or as a congregation, our worship. . .will be unacceptable to God." [9] On the other hand, service cannot be divorced from worship. It is doubtful if our service to our fellowman will be acceptable to God unless it stems from and to some degree is accompanied with worship. Many Christians can testify that some of the most meaningful worship experiences they have had have been as they served others in the name of the Lord. They were conscious, to an unusual degree, of his presence with them in the service.

There is a sense, as implied earlier, that worship is preparatory to service. It must not be treated, however, as merely preparatory or it will cease to serve effectively as preparation for service. Genuine worship, as was true of the experience of the three disciples on the Mount of Transfiguration, is a deeply satisfying experience. It can properly be considered an end within itself and not a means to some other end. In actuality, however, it is an end that points to an end beyond itself. We feel impelled by the presence of the Lord to move from the mountain of worship to serve in the valley filled with human need.

Every vision or unusual awareness of the presence of the Lord, recorded in the Scriptures, included a command to do something about the vision. In other words, it was not only a vision of God but also a vision or command of service for God. To Isaiah it was a question: "Who will go for us" (Isa. 6:8); for Paul it was "Rise and enter the city, and you will be told what you are to do" (Acts 9:6). There was something to be done about the vision.[10] We may not have visions comparable to the visions of the saints of God of the past, but any genuine worship experience will include a command to go and do something about the experience we have had in and with the Lord. At least there will be an inner urge to go out from the worship of God and translate the vision of God we have received into reality in our own lives and in the world.

We may thoroughly disagree with John A. T. Robinson's general theological position, but he has an excellent statement concerning the relation of worship and service. It is as follows: "The test of worship is how far it makes us *more sensitive* to 'the beyond in our midst,' to the Christ in the hungry, the naked, the homeless and the prisoner. Only if we are *more likely* to recognize him there after attending an act of worship is that worship Christian rather than a piece of religiosity in Christian dress." [11]

A church in Tulsa, Oklahoma, has two stained-glass windows that symbolize the proper relation of worship and service. One of those windows, or something comparable to it, is seen in many churches. The other window is unusual. As the people come into the sanctuary they face a cross in the window back of the pulpit. This symbolizes the purpose of the people coming into the sanctuary: they come to worship God. After the worship service, as they turn to leave the church building they face another stained glass window. The most prominent symbol in this window is a yoke. Christians leave the house of God yoked together with one another and with their risen Lord to serve people in his name.

FOR THOUGHT AND DISCUSSION

1. There has been considerable controversy in recent years concerning the relative importance of evangelism and social concern. What is your position? How can the Bible help us relate the two properly? How does one's understanding of the nature of God (Chap. II) relate to this problem? What about the following statements about Jesus: "For the Son of man came to seek and save the lost" (Luke 19:10) and "He went about doing good" (Acts 10:38)? Where has your church been weaker: evangelism or social concern?

2. Charles M. Sheldon wrote a best-selling book a number of years ago entitled *In His Steps.* Some have suggested that a better title would have been *What Would Jesus Have Me to Do?* How would you evaluate these titles? Are they questions that a Christian should ask?

3. Appraise, from the Christian perspective, the following quotations from Hugh Hefner, editor of *Playboy:* "Chastity is just another word for repression; repression is harmful"; "Our democracy. . .has proved in-

tolerably restrictive in matters of sex"; "These sex statutes [laws against fornication and adultery] stand as mute evidence of the extent to which we have failed to live up to the ideal of a free and separate church and state in America."

Also evaluate the following, which he quotes approvingly: "Books, and pictures, and pamphlets and papers that deal openly and honestly with sex have little or no effect upon human behavior. Whatever effect they do have is healthful, rather than injurious to society."

PART II
THE NATURE OF THE
CHRISTIAN LIFE

No one word or term describes adequately the Christian life and its ethic. Several terms that can properly be used provide the basis for the chapter titles in Part II. Each of these is related to some aspect of the Christian life: its motive, its authority, its values, its ideal, and its virtues. A descriptive word is used with each aspect or subject: its *highest* motive, its *ultimate* authority, its *supreme* value, its *comprehensive* ideal, and its *crowning* virtue. These defining words correctly suggest that there may be and are other motives, sources of authority, values, ideals, and virtues.

The subjects for the chapters set forth various aspects of the Christian ethic which has been defined as "an attempt to study and interpret the Christian life." In other words, the Christian ethic is a glory of God ethic, a will of God ethic, a perfectionist ethic, a kingdom of God ethic, and an ethic of love or *agape*. It can also be correctly described as an ethic of the cross (chap. XI), a grace ethic, a commitment ethic, and an ethic of the Holy Spirit. Except for the increased length of the manuscript, each of these could justifiably have been the basis for a chapter. The Christian life, along with the ethic that describes it and gives guidance to it, is so broad, so deep, so complex that many terms are needed to provide a proper understanding and interpretation of it.

VI

Its Highest Motive: Glory of God

Every aspect of the Christian ethic and of the Christian life in general should be God-oriented rather than man-oriented. This God-orientation or God-centeredness in the area of motives can be expressed in various ways. The most inclusive way is to say that the highest motive for the child of God is the desire to glorify God. Some may contend that the glory of God [1] should be considered the goal of life rather than the dominant motive in life. But as a goal it should so possess us that it becomes the controlling motive in our lives. This does not mean that the desire for the glory of God will actually be the dominant motive in every time of decision. Most of what Christians do is prompted by mixed motives. We do believe, however, that the glory of God should be the motive by which all other motives are evaluated. If there is a hierarchy of motives, the glory of God belongs at the apex.

Meaning of "Glory"

The references in the Bible to the glory of God are frequent and varied. It is said that the glory of the Lord filled the tabernacle (Ex. 40:34). There were times when "the glory of the Lord appeared to all the people" (Lev. 9:23; cf. Num. 16:19). Isaiah heard the seraphim singing:

Holy, holy, holy is the Lord of hosts;
  the whole earth is full of his glory.

(Isa. 6:3)

The Psalmist said that "the heavens declare the glory of God" (Ps. 19:1, KJV). People should declare the glory of God and ascribe to him the "glory due his name" (1 Chron. 16:24, 29). When the angel of the Lord appeared to the shepherds to announce the birth of the Messiah "the glory of the Lord shone around them" (Luke 2:9). These are only a few of the many references to the glory of God in both Testaments.

It is doubtful if the glory of God can operate as an effective motive in our lives unless we have a reasonably clear idea of the meaning of "glory." When the children of Israel used the term "the glory of God" they referred primarily to the majesty of God. The Hebrew word *(kabod)*, most frequently translated "glory," carries the idea of weight or mass. But "for the Semite what has weight has importance and value." [2]

An examination of the Scriptures reveals, in the main, two concepts or perspectives concerning the glory of God, both of which are related to and could be derived from the idea of "weight" or "importance and value." The term "the glory of God" was frequently used to refer to some physical phenomenon in or through which the presence of God was manifested. The phenomenon provided the setting or the channel for the revelation of the glory; it was not the glory itself. From this perspective the glory is frequently associated with natural phenomena such as "a devouring fire" (Ex. 24:17) and the lightning and thunder that accompany a storm. It was Ezekiel who said: "And behold, the glory of the God of Israel came from the east; and the sound of his coming was like the sound of many waters; and the earth shone with his glory" (Ezek. 43:2). Evidently the reference was to lightning and thunder. Most frequently the glory is associated with the cloud (see Ex. 16:10; 24:16; 40:34–35), which may suggest that the glory of God was concealed from man and never fully comprehended by him.

The glory was not only revealed, to some degree, in the storm and through the cloud, it was also associated with light. There is radiance in his presence. This is the secret to the shining face of Moses (Ex. 34:29): "he had been talking with God" and something of the glory of God had become his. This was also the secret to the transfiguration of Jesus, which, according to Luke, took place as he prayed (Luke 9:29). Also, Moses and Elijah "appeared in glory" (v. 31) and the three disciples "saw his [Christ's] glory" (v. 32). Saul was stricken blind on the Damascus road by the brilliance of the light which accompanied the appearance of the glorified living Christ (Acts 9:3–9). It is no wonder that the writer of Revelation says that the new Jersusalem "has no need of sun or moon to shine upon it, for the glory of God is its light" (Rev. 21:23).

In addition to the manifestation of the glory of God through natural phenomena, his glory is also associated with and revealed by his "moral excellence" or character. For example, when Moses asked God to show him his glory, the Lord said, "I will make all my goodness pass before you. . .I will be gracious, and will show mercy on whom I will show mercy" (Ex. 33:19). This aspect of the glory of God may not be self-evident as that which can be revealed by means of natural phenomena, but it is present and is particularly important for any study of the Christian life. It is possible that these two aspects of the glory of God are not as mutually exclusive as the preceding might imply. God's radiance and splendor are most fully revealed by his character, and in the final analysis, they are dependent on what he is.

A clue to the meaning of "glory" *(doxa)* from the New Testament perspective can be found by the words with which "glory" is linked or associated. It is associated most frequently with honor (see Rom. 2:10; Heb. 3:3; 1 Peter 1:7; 2 Peter 1:17; and numerous references in Revelation) and power (see Rev. 4:11; 7:12; 15:8; 19:1). When associated with power, the glory evidently refers to something inherent in God. When associated with honor it refers primarily to the attitude that men should have toward him. One reason for honoring or glorifying God is his power or glory.

Rewards and the Glory of God

While the glory of God should be the highest or supreme motive for the child of God, there is a place for lower or secondary motives. Many of us are too immature for the glory of God to serve as the only motive and even in some cases the most effective motive in our lives. This justifies, if it does not actually necessitate, an appeal to more than one type of motive. There is a continuing place, but it is hoped a decreasing place, for an appeal to fear of punishment and expectation of reward.

There is considerable evidence of such appeals in the Scriptures. For example, God said to Abram: "Fear not, Abram, I am your shield; your reward shall be very great" (Gen. 15:1). The Psalmist said that in the keeping of the precepts and ordinances of the Lord "there is a great reward" (Ps. 19:11). Such a prudential appeal is particularly prevalent in the wisdom literature of the Old Testament. The general or orthodox position among the Jews was that the good or righteous man prospered. In contrast, suffering or personal misfortune was an evidence of God's displeasure. This perspective provides the background for an understanding of the approach of Job's friends to his problems. Job's suffering, from their viewpoint, was an evidence of God's displeasure because of his sins. They contended that he should confess his sins and make things right with God. The close relation of righteousness and reward is spelled out with particular clarity in Proverbs, where it is said; "One who sows righteousness gets a sure reward" (Prov. 11:18). Also,

> The reward for humility and fear of the Lord is riches and honor and life.
>
> (Prov. 22:4)

It should be noticed, however, that these and other references in the Old Testament are, in the main, simple statements of fact. God is not under obligation to give a reward. Whatever is given is of grace.

There are similar statements of fact, with at least an implied motivation, in the teachings of Jesus. The beatitudes are examples: the blessings are the natural results of the virtues. Jesus also said that one who gives his alms and fasts secretly will be rewarded (Matt. 6:4, 18). Again, he said that one who gives a cup of cold water to one of the little ones "shall not lose his reward" (Matt. 10:42). The main thing from the perspective of our study is that the cup of cold water, which was a proverbial expression for minor or relatively insignificant service, was not motivated by the desire for reward. Here as elsewhere the reward was "not set forth as the motive for right conduct," rather "a certain type of conduct will bring its own reward." [3]

There was at least one occasion when Peter, possibly representing the disciples, asked Jesus about a reward. Peter's statement and question were: "Lo, we have left everything and followed you. What then shall we have?" (Matt. 19:27; cf. Mk. 10:28; Lk. 18:28). In reply to the question, which is specifically stated only in Matthew, Jesus said that they would be abundantly rewarded "in this time" "with persecutions" and "in the age to come eternal life" (Mark and Luke). It has been suggested that this is the only occasion when Jesus promised a reward in this life. [4] And notice that even here the final point of reference is to the life to come.

Jesus frequently promised a reward or stated that a reward would follow a certain action or attitude. It seems, however, that the reward would come only to those who were prepared to follow him and to do what was right on the basis of a motive other than reward. An example of this is what he said concerning losing and saving life. The promise is reserved for those who lose their lives for his sake (Matt. 16:25).

There were times when Jesus called for service without reference to reward (Lk. 9:57–62; 14:25–33). Many of his parables limited, if they did not eliminate, the idea of reward (Matt. 20:1–16; Lk. 17:7–10). In the judgment scene (Matt. 25:31–36) those on the right hand were rewarded but they were unaware of their service. This meant that the expectation of a reward could not have been their motive. Really, in most cases where a reward is mentioned or implied by Jesus, it comes as a natural, inevitable consequence. In other words, it is simply how things actually work. For example, Jesus on more than one occasion said: "He who humbles himself will be exalted" (Matt. 23:12; Lk. 14:ll; 18:14). Was Jesus using this as a basis for an appeal to humility, or was he simply stating a fact? It seems clear that it was the latter. Selfish, self-seeking "humility" would not be real humility. One thing that true humility requires is a forgetting of self. Again, Jesus said, "If any one would be first, he must be last of all and servant of all" (Mk. 9:35). But can one become first by deliberately becoming servant of all with the expectation that this will make him first? No, the service must be rendered without any motive beyond the service itself except as that motive moves us toward God and the glory of God. Generally speaking, when a Christian does a thing for the sake of a reward, he will not be rewarded. Self-seeking service is self-defeating. C. S. Lewis says that "the proper rewards are not simply tacked on the activity for which they are given, but are the activity itself in consummation." [5]

There is some evidence in the Pauline epistles of an emphasis on both punishment and reward (Rom. 2:1–11; 14:10–12; 2 Cor. 5:10). His moral exhortations are accompanied with threats and promises (Gal. 5:21; 1 Cor. 6:9). He himself runs the Christian race like a contestant in a race seeking to win the prize (1 Cor. 9:24–27). In a few places Paul refers to rewards that come in the present life (see 2 Cor. 9:6ff.; Eph. 6:2–3; Phil. 4:17–19), although in most places the reference is to rewards in the next life. In Paul, as was true of Jesus, in most places where the idea of reward is used, it is simply a statement of fact, a certain type of conduct will bring its own reward.

The New Testament perspective in general is that any reward that one may receive is of grace and not of merit. Salvation is a gift of God and the blessings that come to the saved are also gifts from God. God is not a debtor to those who do good works. Rather, men, because of the grace of God, are debtors to him. The good we do is not an achievement that merits a reward. Rather, it evolves from our inner realtionship with the resurrected Christ. This relationship and what flows from it are results of the working of God's grace. Out of gratitude to God for what he has done and what he does for us, we should seek to glorify him by the quality of life we live for him.

There is a sense in which the glory that is God's is our chief source of inspiration, while at the same time the promotion of his glory among men is our highest motivation. This highest or purest of all motives will become increasingly dominant in our lives as we mature in our union with Christ. And interestingly, the more mature we become as children of God the less conscious we will be that we are seeking to live for the glory of God. What Carpenter says about Christian virtue could be said concerning life in general of the mature Christian. He says, "Christian virtue. . .has about it something of the effortless ease of a great work of art." [6] Such "effortless ease" is evident in the lives of God's saints. Not many of us, however, would claim that we have reached that stage yet. We see it as an ideal toward which to move. One factor that will move us in that direction is to set our faces toward the glory that is the Lord's. Paul, writing to the Corinthians, said, "And we all, with unveiled face, beholding the glory of the Lord, are being changed into his likeness from one degree of glory to another" (2 Cor. 3:18). The reference is to an essential, a real, or an inner change in contrast to a change of external appearance. The change is continuous but never complete until the end of the journey when we shall awake in his likeness. As Ramsey says, "There is no despair, for glory is a present possession: there is no contentment, for a far greater glory is the final goal." [7] Also, the more thoroughly we are "changed. . .from one degree of glory to another," the more we will glorify God. In turn, the more the glory of God becomes the dominant motive in our lives the more the glory that is his will become an integral, meaningful part of our lives.

Christian Conduct and the Glory of God

"The role of glory in Christian conduct is of primary importance." [8] There is or should be a basic difference in the good "conduct" or good works of Christians and non-Christians. The fundamental motive of the former should be the glory of God; of the latter on its highest level it is the well-being of man.

Jesus admonished his disciples as follows: "Even so let your light shine before men; that they may see your good works, and glorify your Father who is in heaven" (Matt. 5:16). A light does not shine to call attention to itself. It shines that others may be seen. The Christian does not carry a light; he *is* a light, the light of the world. Also, his is not a reflected light, such as the moon. His is an inner light, derived from his union with the One who is the Light of the World. The light we have comes from God, belongs to him. It should be used to glorify him. We shine only to the degree that we permit the Divine Inner Light to touch and transform our lives. The more fully we let that Light permeate our lives the more we will produce good works. Also, as we mature in our experience in and with the resurrected Christ, who is that Inner Light, the more completely whatever good works we produce will glorify God rather than be produced for our own personal glory. As this is true, others will increasingly understand the real source of the light that produces the good works in our lives. Furthermore, the more they recognize the True Light that lighteth every man that cometh into the world, the more they will glorify or praise God.

It may be wise to suggest that when men glorify God, they do not add to his glory. His glory is complete or perfect. Even the best and most mature of men, however, can never completely comprehend the glory of God. As we put the glory of God first in our lives, we will understand more fully the nature of that glory. Also, by the light revealed by the good works of Christians, others will be enabled to recognize more clearly the nature of the glory and will be led to praise, honor, or glorify God. Ramsey, referring to Israel, says that Israel could give God glory and "set forth his glory among the nations only if Israel is herself a people in whose conduct He is glorified." [9] This statement can be adapted and applied to the new Israel. We can "set forth" God's glory among the peoples with whom we have contact only as we glorify him in our conduct.

Another way of expressing the same idea is to say that we glorify God by living a fruitful life. In the great vine and branches statement Jesus said: "By this my Father is glorified, that you bear much fruit, and so prove to be my disciples" (John 15:8). Williams, typically bringing out the

verb tense, translates the verse as follows: "By your continuously bearing abundant fruit and in this way proving
yourself to be real disciples of mine, my Father is glorified."
Notice the "*is* glorified." This is timeless: any time we bear
fruit we glorify the Father. And the more abundant the fruit
we bear, the more our lives will glorify God. Also, it can
wisely be repeated over and over again that the yield depends on how thoroughly we abide in him or how fully we
let him live in us. Furthermore, since our abiding in him is
not perfect or complete, the increase is seldom if ever "a
hundredfold" or possibly even "sixtyfold." It is in this sense
as well as from other perspectives that "a Christian never
'is,' but always 'is becoming' a Christian." But whether the
increase is thirtyfold, sixtyfold, or a hundredfold, the fruitfulness of the Christian indicates or proves his claim to be
a disciple of Christ.

But what is meant by "fruit" and "fruitbearing"? It
seems that "fruit" refers to the qualities of life that people
associate with God. As we bear the fruit of dependability,
holiness, justice, righteousness, impartiality, love, and other
qualities that men attribute to God, such fruit glorifies him.
This makes fruit bearing closely related to the every-day
decisions and issues of life.

Paul, in discussing the eating of meat offered to idols,
said, "Whether you eat or drink or whatever you do, do all
to the glory ["honour," NEB] of God" (1 Cor. 10:31). The
"whatever" and "do all" make this statement by Paul an
inclusive guideline for life and for life's daily decisions. It
represents for the Christian the highest possible motive. We
may fall short of measuring up to it, but we should all agree
that it should be the ultimate ideal of our lives. It should
be the standard by which we would measure all other standards.

There are many other direct and indirect references in
the Pauline epistles and elsewhere in the New Testament to

the glory of God as the goal and motive of the Christian life. For example, since the body is "for the Lord," is a member of Christ, "is a temple of the Holy Spirit," it is to be used to glorify God (1 Cor. 6:13, 15, 19, 20). Paul also said that the offering for the saints at Jerusalem was for the glory of God (2 Cor. 9:13). He appealed to the Philippians to be "filled with the fruits of righteousness which come through Christ, to the glory and praise of God" (Phil. 1:11). Notice two things: source—"through Christ," and purpose—"to the glory and praise of God." Paul made a statement to the Ephesians that can appropriately apply to us today although the immediate reference was evidently to Jews like himself: "We. . .have been destined and appointed to live for the praise of his glory" (Eph. 1:12).

There is an exhortation in First Peter that summarizes the place of the glory of God as a motive in the Christian life. After suggesting that "as each has received a gift, employ it for one another, as good stewards of God's varied grace" (1 Pet. 4:10), he then says that "whoever speaks" and "whoever renders service" should do so "that in everything God may be glorified through Jesus Christ." He then breaks out in a doxology: "To him belong glory and dominion for ever and ever. Amen" (1 Pet. 4:11). Notice the inclusive "in everything," which is comparable to Paul's "whatever you do" (1 Cor. 10:31). As *Interpreter's Bible* says, Peter "sums up all that he has tried to say. The end, as well as the dynamic of it all is *that in everything God may be glorified through Jesus Christ."*

Peter even suggests that those to whom he wrote should rejoice in so far as they shared in the suffering of Christ, knowing that they will also rejoice "when his glory is revealed" (1 Pet. 4:13). Furthermore, if they suffer as Christians, let them not be ashamed but let them glorify God (1 Pet. 4:16).

The Cross and the Glory of God

Although the cross will be discussed more fully in a later chapter, at least a brief statement should be made concerning the relation of the cross, which is suffering voluntarily accepted and redemptive in purpose, to the glory of God. Jesus closely related his suffering on the cross to his own glory and to the glory of God. This was particularly true in the closing conversations he had with his disciples as recorded in the last chapters of John's Gospel. To the Greeks, to Andrew and Philip who had brought the Greeks to him and possibly to the other disciples, Jesus said: "The hour has come for the Son of Man to be glorified" (John 12:23). What is meant by "the hour" and how was he to be glorified?

He evidently had been conscious for some time of a particularly significant hour or time that awaited him. It is evident in the preceding reference in John 12 and elsewhere that "the hour" referred to his crucifixion, along with his resurrection and subsequent ascension. Immediately after the statement to the Greeks and others, Jesus asked and answered a very significant question. The question, "And what shall I say, 'Father, save me from this hour'?" The answer, "No, for this purpose I have come to this hour" (John 12:7). His marvelous prayer, recorded in John 17, opens with a triumphant note: "He lifted up his eyes to heaven and said, 'Father, the hour has come; glorify thy Son that the Son may glorify thee' "(John 17:1). In the Garden of Gethsemane he quietly said just before his betrayal, "The hour is at hand" (Matt. 26:45).

The cross and the glory were not only closely related in the life of Jesus; they are also closely related in the lives of his followers. The resurrected Christ revealed to Peter that when he was old he would stretch out his hands and another would bind him fast (NEB) and carry him where he did not wish to go. Then in parentheses it is said, "This he said to show by what death he was to glorify God" (John 21:18–19). It was at the tomb of Lazarus that Jesus said to Martha: "Did I not tell you that if you would believe you would see the glory of God" (John 11:40). He had previously told his disciples that the illness of Lazarus was "for the glory of God" (John 11:4).

Some may contend that the real glory is in the coming forth from the grave and not in the death. The power of God was demonstrated and his glory was revealed when Jesus called Lazarus forth from the grave. But Lazarus could not have come forth if he had not previously died. In other words, there is no resurrection without crucifixion, but there is no real crucifixion without resurrection. It should be remembered, however, that the Christian crucifixion is basically the cruicifixion of self with selfish ambitions, motives, and purposes. This means that there cannot be any element of self-centeredness in a real cruicifixion. We cannot premeditatively say that we will crucify self that we may be resurrected to a more glorious life. We cannot give life for the purpose of discovering life. There must be a real giving if there is to be a real discovery. This is another place where it is necessary for us to speak in relative terms. To the degree that we crucify self, to that degree and that degree only will we really find life. Only to that degree will we glorify God. And the purpose of real crucifixion or of a real taking up of a cross is the glory of God.

The Future Glory

The glory of God that we can share through our fellowship with him is never complete in this life. We "are being changed ("transfigured," NEB) into his likeness from one degree of glory to another" (2 Cor. 3:18). The change takes place as we behold "the glory of the Lord." The word translated "changed" here and "transformed" in Romans 12:1 is the same word in the Greek that is used for the transfiguration of Jesus (Matt. 17:2; Mk. 9:2). It is the word from which we get our English word metamorphose and related words. We are changed from one degree of glory to another or "in ever-increasing splendour into His own image" (Ph.) by looking to him, or better, by abiding in him and letting him abide in us. Our abiding, however, is never perfect, and hence we never attain the full likeness or the complete glory. It is Christ within us that is our hope of glory in the future (Col. 1:27) but also our hope of glory now and our only hope of moving from one degree of glory to another.

Likewise, the child of God can never in this life comprehend fully the glory that is the Lord's. There will come a time when we will behold his glory in its fullness. We believe we were included in that marvelous prayer Jesus prayed for his disciples. One of the most meaningful petitions in that prayer was as follows: "Father, I desire that they also, whom thou hast given me, may be with me where I am." Then notice the reason or motive: "to behold my glory which thou has given me in thy love for me before the foundation of the world" (John 17:24). The expectation of beholding his glory and sharing, to some degree, in that glory should make a tremendous appeal to anyone who has become a child of God through faith in Christ.

Paul and Peter both made appeals to the future as they sought to lead people to live for Christ. For example, Peter said, "Maintain good conduct among the Gentiles ("pagans" NEB), so that in case they speak against you as wrongdoers, they may see your good deeds and glorify God on the day of visitation" ("in the judgment day," Wm.) (1 Pet. 2:12): "one saintly life is worth a dozen stout volumes on Christian apologetics" *(Interpreter's Bible)*. Paul says that "the sufferings of this present time are not worth comparing with the glory that is to be revealed to us ("which is in store for us," NEB) (Rom. 8:18). Paul goes further and says that "this slight momentary affliction is preparing for us an eternal weight of glory beyond all comparison" (2 Cor. 4:17). Phillips translates the verse as follows: "These little troubles (which are really so transitory) are winning for us a permanent and glorious reward out of all proportion to our pain." It is possible that Paul meant this as a simple statement of fact rather than as an appeal. Even if this were the case, it should operate in our lives as a tremendously strong motive. If we are faithful as children of God, there awaits us "an eternal weight of glory" or a "glorious reward."

In conclusion, let us suggest again that reward has a place in Christian motivation. We do believe, however, that the highest motive is and the dominant motive should be the glory of God. In the final analysis "the glorious reward" awaiting the child of God is inevitably related to the glory of God. Only those who have unselfishly sought to glorify God in this life will receive or know the eternal weight of glory in the next life. Deeds that are done with personal reward as the primary motive find their reward in this life and not the next. After all, the most glorious thing for the child of God will be to be in the presence of God, singing the song of Moses and the Lamb, and beholding the glory of the One who has redeemed him.

FOR THOUGHT AND DISCUSSION

1. Can one succeed in business, in the professions, in politics and be a dedicated Christian? Can he have as his primary motive the glory of God? What place can a desire for promotion or advancement have in his life? What about the profit motive? Can it be made compatible with a desire to glorify God?

2. Examine a recent decision you have made: to make a

trip, to visit a relative or friend, to accept a responsibility in church or community, to change your job or work, to give to a worthy cause—church or community. It may have been a decision known by others or only by you and God. Was the decision consciously and deliberately made, or did you simply drift into it or respond to strong pressure? What factors entered into the decision? How much were you motivated selfishly? How much consideration did you give to the well-being of others—family and friends? How much were you prompted by gratitude to God and a desire to honor him?

3. What is the relation of the glory of God as motive to the will of God as the source of authority in our lives (discussed in the next chapter)? Will we glorify God to the degree that we accept his will as the supreme authority in our lives?

VII

Its Ultimate Authority: The Will of God

Those with widely divergent theological and ethical positions usually agree that the ultimate or final source of authority for the child of God is the will of God. Differences arise, however, in regard to how one can know the will of God or the source or sources for an authoritative word concerning the content of the will of God. Some of the major answers have been "an infallible tradition," "an infallible book" (the Bible), "an infallible institution" (the church), "an infallible leader or person" (the priest), or "an infallible experience." Some Christians so magnify the non-Christian elements, particularly reason, that their approach becomes more philosophical and secular than distinctly Christian. For most Christians, however, authority rests in God and his will rather than in man and his reason. They believe, and rightly so, that the most important thing any Christian can do is to seek to know the will of God and once knowing it to do it. As Bonhoeffer says, "The only appropriate conduct of men before God is the doing of His will." The continuing question of the child of God is or should be the one Zedekiah asked Jeremiah: "Is there any word from the Lord'" (Jer. 37:17). This is true whether the question or issue is in the area of personal morality such as sex outside of marriage—before or after—divorce and remarriage, or some broader social issue such as the relative importance of law, order, and justice or the best kind of welfare program for the needy.

The Nature of the Will of God

The will of God evolves from and is expressive of the nature of God. This means that the ultimate source of authority for the Christian is God himself. Since he is the sovereign God of the universe his will is inclusive of the totality of our lives. He has a will for us in every time of decision. This has tremendous significance for us in the area of every-day Christian living. He also has a will for the family, the church, the community, the nation, and the world.

The will of God is so broad that some defining objectives are needed to describe it accurately. Among some descriptive defining words that have been applied to the will of God are "perfect" and "permissive," "ideal" and "interim." In addition, there are Leslie Weatherhead's well-known distinctions between what he calls the ultimate, intentional, and circumstantial will of God. The last two of these are of particular significance in a study of the Christian life. The Christian should seek to know in every time of decision the perfect, ideal, or intentional will of God. He discovers, however, that most decisions differ to some degree from all previous decisions. Past decisions may suggest some guide lines for the present, but each decision is usually related to a particular set of circumstances. This means that in most times of decision we seek God's circumstantial will.

Also, there will be occasions when we will be relatively certain of the intentional or perfect will of God and yet it will seem or actually be impossible to follow it. For example, there are times when doing the will of God depends not only on our willingness but also on the willingness of others. A young couple may have a deep conviction that it is God's will for them to go to the foreign mission field, but

their Foreign Mission Board may say "No." It is recognized, of course, that the couple could be wrong, but not
necessarily so. The Board, composed of men and women
with their limitations, might be wrong. The couple can be
sure, however, that God has a will for them in the new
circumstances of life. As Paul Tournier says, "At every
moment, no matter what the accumulated ruins may be,
there is a plan of God to be found." Or, stated somewhat
differently, Bonhoeffer says, "Through every event, however untoward, there is always a way through to God," and
hence a way through to his will.

The idea of the circumstantial will of God is closely
related to the lesser-of-two-evils theory concerning moral
decisions. Since we are evil and the world in which we live
is evil, frequently our decisions are not between an unmixed
good and an unmixed evil, between white and black, but
are in the gray area. The best one can do is to make the
decision that will result in the maximum of good and the
minimum of evil, recognizing that on many occasions some
evil will result whatever the decision may be. As long as it
is clearly recognized that the decision is the lesser-of-two
evils, it will not do a great deal of damage. There will remain
a tug toward the greater good, or toward the intentional or
perfect will of God. As long as the tug is there, there is hope
for improvement. This means that the circumstantial will of
God, when properly understood, will tend to move us toward his intentional will.

Another distinction that is frequently made that is closely related to the intentional and circumstantial will of God
is the difference between the absolute and the relative. The
choice here, as is so frequently true, is not an either/or but
a both/and. There is not only a place in the Christian life
for both the relative and the absolute; they really belong
together. Tillich, for example, suggests that "basic ethical
norms must unite an absolute element and a relative el-

ement. They must be universally valid and, at the same time, adapted to the concrete situation." [1] Their adaptation does not nullify their universal validity. One absolute, operative for the Christian in every particular situation, is his submission to God and his obedience to the will of God. The more completely we follow the will of God, the more clearly we will understand that it is "good and acceptable and perfect" (Rom. 12:2). We will discover that his will is always best for us.

The Bible and the Will of God

Whether we are considering the intentional or the circumstantial will of God, we still need to know how we can know his will. How can man know what God is seeking to say to him? How has God sought to speak to men in the past, and how does he attempt to speak to them today? What channels does he use to reveal his will to us? These questions correctly imply, as suggested earlier, that we believe that the final authoritative word for the child of God is in God and his will. Right for us is basically not what reason dictates but what God says. It is not what society or any segment of society approves but what our heavenly Father approves.

God through the centuries has sought to reveal his will to men through nature, through providence, and through history. These sources for the will of God have been and are helpful, but they do not provide sufficient guidance. In addition to this general revelation there is a special or unique revelation which is recorded in the Scriptures. The Bible is the main tangible, objective source for a knowledge of God and his will. When we agree that this is true, there still remain some questions concerning the Bible that need to be answered.

One question is: is the Bible the only source for a knowledge of the will of God? The answer is clearly, No. It is a unique source for the will of God, but it is not the exclusive source. The reasons for this answer will become evident as we proceed with our discussion. Another question is: what about problems, and there are many, that are not directly discussed or considered in the Bible? What is the source of authority for the Christian then? Still another question is: what about portions of the Bible that require interpretation? Who is to speak the authoritative word for the child of God? These questions will be discussed, to some extent, later.

The following question is one that we will not discuss later: is all the Bible equally authoritative, equally a source for the will of God? There are some who contend that all of the Bible, Old Testament and New Testament, is equally authoritative. This was the viewpoint, in the main, of the reformers, the Puritan fathers, and is the viewpoint of many today. Many who hold this position become what might be called "Old Testament Christians." Their perspective, in the main, is the perspective of the Old Testament rather than of the New. They have not moved from Law to Grace. They need to remember the words of Jesus, "You have heard that it was said. . .but I say unto you. . ." (Matt. 5:21, 27, 33, 39, 43).

Others suggest that authority rests primarily in the New Testament. An Old Testament scholar (II. II. Rowley) says that the New Testament must be finally normative for the Christian even in his understanding of the Old Testament. The Old Testament forms a unity with the New Testament, but to use a term of Rowley's, it is a dynamic rather than a static unity. There is movement.

A third viewpoint is that the final authority for the Christian rests in the life and teachings of Jesus. It is the writer of Hebrews who says, "In many and various ways God spoke of old to our fathers by the prophets, but in these last days he has spoken to us by a Son." That Son "reflects the glory of God and bears the very stamp of his nature" (Heb. 1:1–3). The climax of the revelation of the nature, character, and will of God is in the Son. This means that Christ is the final authority rather than the Bible as such. The authority, in the final analysis, is not in the words of the Scriptures but in *the Word* revealed in the Scriptures which produced the Scriptures and which also makes them come alive. The Scriptures can lead us to Christ but, as sacred as they are, they cannot take the place of Christ. When properly understood, this does not detract from the authority of the Bible, it clarifies and deepens it. Back of the Bible is the divine Person who gave birth to the Bible. His authority is prior to the Bible, but it is also expressed through the Bible.

Some people suggest that only those elements of the teachings of Jesus that have passed the test of historical-textual criticism should be considered authoritative. Many who take this position look for authority outside of the Bible. They tend to make a purely rational or philosophical approach even though they may speak and write about the Christian life and the Christian ethic. This should not be interpreted as belittling the historical-textual approach. Anything that will help to get us closer to the original manuscripts should be welcomed.

The Holy Spirit and the Will of God

The Bible, as suggested, is the main tangible, objective source for a knowledge of the will of God. The Holy Spirit is the main inner subjective source for such a knowledge. Both the Scriptures and the guidance of the Holy Spirit are needed in man's search for an authoritative word from the Lord. They do not contradict one another, although because of our human limitations they may seem to at times. They speak the same word because they both speak of and for *the Word* made flesh. In general, the Scriptures speak *of* Christ, the Spirit speaks *for* Christ. The unity of their authority rests in Christ.

It is also true that the Holy Spirit speaks in and through the Scriptures. He as the inspirer of the writers of the Scriptures is the best interpreter of those Scriptures. He illuminates the words of the Scriptures, making them come alive. To paraphrase a statement of Henlee Barnette's: To be guided by the Spirit is to be led into a knowledge of the will of God as revealed in the Scriptures and climaxed in Christ.[2] While the Spirit does not contradict the Scriptures, he does at times supplement them. When the Christian finds no direct word from the Lord in the Scriptures that will help in a particular situation, he then can seek the guidance of the Spirit. Both Scriptures and the Holy Spirit are needed. Brunner concludes that "as the Scriptures without the Spirit produces false legalism, . . .so the Spirit without the Scriptures produces false Antinomianism, and fanaticism." [3]

The clarity of our insight into the Scriptures and into the will of God will be determined, to a considerable degree, by our willingness to be led by the Holy Spirit. He has been sent into the world to teach us all things (John 14:26). It is only the seeking mind and the willing heart, however, that will know: "If any man's will is to do his will, he shall know. . ." (John 7:17). At best, our knowledge of God and his will is never complete or perfect. The will of God is never static, not only because of our human limitations but also because it is the will of the *living* God. Furthermore, the Christian is constantly faced with new situations involving varying circumstances. The will of God for man is not a mere abstraction. It is a dynamic reality which must find expression in constantly changing situations.

The maturing Christian acknowledges not only that his knowledge of the will of God is far from perfect; he also admits that many times he lacks the desire to know that will. Even when he knows the will of God he frequently lacks the dynamic to move him toward the attainment of that will. In other words, the child of God is in desperate need of the guidance and the power of the Holy Spirit.[4]

The Church and the Will of God

The Holy Spirit not only speaks to the individual child of God, he also speaks in, to, and through the Christian fellowship. Any Christian should consider very seriously the judgment of his church. Some churches and some Christians claim that the final word of God even for the individual Christian is channeled through the church. They suggest that the church is the mediator of the will of God.

Those who take this position may agree that the Bible is a record of God's will for man, but they claim that the people of God antedated the Bible, gave birth to it, and hence the authority rests primarily in the church. It is contended that the Bible should be considered authoritative only as it is interpreted by the church.

It is true that the Bible is in a sense the product of the people or community of God. In the Old Testament this community was the Chosen People. They produced the books of the Old Testament. Those books, to a considerable degree, grew out of their experiences with God. In the New Testament the Church, the spiritual Israel, gave birth to the books of the New Testament.

The books of the New Testament as well as those of the Old Testament cannot be understood fully, interpreted properly, or applied wisely apart from an understanding of the historic situation that gave them birth. The Bible is a record of God's activity in, through, and on behalf of his people. It reveals God at work within the historic process speaking to a particular day but we believe expressing truths that are applicable to every day.

Does this mean that the final source of authority is the church or the people of God? Let us consider for a moment the Old Testament. Back of the people of God was God himself. They cannot be explained apart from him and his purposes. The revelation of God which gave birth to the Old Testament may have been and was given to his people, but we should remember that it was given and not invented by them. Also, it was given to them that they might share it with others. In other words, the people of God were created by the revelation rather than creators of the revelation.

Something of the same relation can be seen in the New Testament. It is true that the church preceded the Scriptures and gave rise to them. However, the Christian community or church is explained by something outside or beyond itself. That something was the Divine Event, the pivotal point of all history: the life, death, and resurrection of Christ. This event gave birth both to the church and to the New Testament Scriptures. It is true that the church ultimately formulated and determined the canon, but the books of the New Testament were not originated by the church.

John Knox suggests that rather paradoxically the Bible is, on the one hand, less than the church and, on the other hand, it is greater than the church "because it brings us the only record we have of the event through which the community was brought into being and therefore provides the only means for its constant renewal." He then adds: "This is the ground of the Bible's authority." [5] The Bible provides the standard and norm even for the church. This is true because of the Divine Event revealed in the Bible which gave birth to the New Testament and also to the church. With Christ as the mediator between God and man, there is no need or room for a mediatorial church. He through the Spirit speaks the final and authoritative word to the child of God. He may use channels or instruments, including the church, but the word is from him, and in the final analysis, he speaks directly to the mind and heart of the believer. The church can and should help men to know the will of God. It, at least, should "tilt men's faces" toward God.

The Individual and the Will of God

When we discussed the Bible as the source of authority two questions were asked that were not answered. Those questions were: what about problems that are not directly discussed or considered in the Bible? What about portions of the Bible that require interpretation? When faced with such situations, who or what is to determine the authoritative word for the child of God? What is the answer to the latter question? We believe that the child of God is not to look to the church or a representative of the church for the final authoritative word. Although the traditions and the teachings of the church should be taken seriously, the individual must finally determine for himself what the will of God is in and for his life. He is the ultimate interpreter of the Bible and of the leadership of the Divine Spirit.

As one seeks to use the Bible in his search for the will of God there are some questions he should ask and seek to answer. Should the Bible be considered a rule book, with a specific solution for every problem, an answer for every question? Are any of its commandments authoritative for us today, except the commandment of love as the situationists insist? Are we justified in setting aside every commandment or principle if the situation seems to justify it? In other words, is the Bible relevant and authoritative for contemporary Christians?[6] This is a tremendously important question and one which every Christian, in a very real sense, must answer sooner or later.

Let us again emphasize that the individual Christian is to

read and interpret the Bible for himself and to apply it to his own life. When he faces problems where he does not find direct guidance in the Bible, he is to decide for himself under the guidance of the Holy Spirit what is the will of God. This is his inherent right as a human created in the image of God. Let us never forget, however, that every right is accompanied with a comparable responsibility. How wonderful is the right we have to live our own lives, to make our own decisions, but how awesome and sometimes terrible is the responsibility.

We should be grateful to our heavenly Father that he has provided many possible sources of help for us as we seek his will. Some of these are human sources, others are more specifically divine sources. Whether human or divine they are good gifts from God. Among the human resources are our own rational nature and what we call "conscience." Reason is a valuable asset to us as we seek to know the will of God. The authority, however, is in the will of God and not in reason or any other source we use to discover that will.

There are other human resources that we can utilize in times of decision. One of these is the counsel or advice of others. This may be counsel that is given personally or through pamphlets and books; it may be counsel that is sought or unsought, given consciously or unconsciously. We can also receive help by participating in the life and work of the church.

A proper use of our personal experiences can help us in our search for the will of God. Some would make experience authoritative. Personal experience may and will help us to interpret and evaluate the truth, but it is not the source of the truth. It is true, however, that the will of God which is external to man never becomes effectively authoritative for him until it is internalized. To become a dynamic reality, it must be experienced.

In addition to the Bible there are other divine resources. One of the most significant of these is prayer, which is communication or dialogue and not monologue. We need to pray as we seek to follow our own best judgment and as we seek the counsel of others. Prayer helps us in many direct and indirect ways. We need to pray not only that we may know the will of God but that we may have the strength and courage to do it.

Another divine resource, previously discussed, is the promise of the leadership of the Holy Spirit. We should seek his leadership as we study the Bible, as we counsel with others, and as we use various resources that are available in seeking to know the will of God. Very seldom does the Spirit flood our soul with light but we can be sure that he will give us enough light to take the next necessary step. There is a Chinese proverb that a journey of a thousand miles begins with one step. We need just enough light to take the next step. The best assurance of being within God's will tomorrow is to be within his will today.

The Situation and the Will of God

There is a great deal of interest in the contemporary period in situation ethics.[7] It is unfortunate that the word "situation" has become identified with this particular type of Christian ethic. This makes it difficult for one to give the proper recognition to the importance of the situation without being considered an advocate of situation ethics. We believe that the situation is an important factor in Christian decision making, but there is much in situation ethics with which we disagree.

The importance of the situation is clearly evident in the Scriptures. A striking example, and one that is cited by some situationalists is Paul's instructions concerning the eating of meat offered to idols (Rom. 14, I Cor. 8, and portions of 9 and 10). Paul plainly said that there was nothing wrong as such with eating the meat but the situation at Rome, Corinth, and evidently elsewhere made the eating of the meat positively wrong or sinful. One thing that should be noted by situationalists and by all of us is that Paul was not talking about an activity that was wrong within itself. The situation, particularly the attitude or reactions of people, may make wrong that which is right within itself, but it can never make right that which is wrong within itself. And we should never forget that Paul and the Scriptures in general considered some things wrong within themselves, including some that at least some proponents of situation ethics claim could be right in certain situations, such as adultery and homosexuality.

Let us repeat, however, that the situation is an important factor in decision making. God's will is made known to us in a concrete situation. As Brunner says, "The Good consists in always doing what God wills at any particular moment." [8] The authority is in God's will. In other words, the authoritative word comes from outside the situation, although God may speak specifically through and to the particular situation.

There is a sense in which the present situation is expressive of and, to some degree, a product of the past. Each situation may be and is unique but never completely so. It has a history. There is a degree of continuity from one situation to another and hence from one decision to another decision. This means, among other things, that wisdom for the present decision may come from and be informed by past events and previous decisions.

The Bible, as a record of God's past dealings with and will for man, has an important word to speak to us in our times of decision. Its precepts and principles are abidingly relevant. Even its laws can and will speak a helpful word if properly interpreted and applied. Barth suggests that the divine law in the Bible is always a concrete command. He further says, "What God commanded and forbade others, He now commands and forbids us. . . . We are to be in every sense the contemporaries of these men." [9] One reason we are the contemporaries of the men of the past is because the God of the past who spoke to them is the God of the present who speaks to us. He speaks to us in the present situation, but he also speaks to us in and through the situations of men of the past. While every decision may be situationally conditioned, it is not situationally determined.

Summary

Let us restate the general position that has been suggested:

The will of God is the source of authority for the child of God in all of the decisions of life.

The individual child of God in any time of decision has the right and the responsibility to decide for himself what the will of God is.

God has given the individual some native equipment such as his judgment or common sense and his conscience or sense of oughtness, that he can and should use as he seeks to know what is the will of God. Other human resources are also available.

There are two major divine resources for a knowledge of the will of God: the Bible (objective) and the Holy Spirit (subjective). Some would make the church a third source. While the church is an important interpreter of what both the Bible and the Spirit have to say, it is never superior or even equal to either of them.

Since the individual, even the redeemed individual, is not only finite but is also sinful, he should maintain an attitude of tentativeness or openmindedness in his interpretation of the will of God. Ours should be a constant process of asking, seeking, knocking that we may know more fully his will in every changing situation.

This means that the situation is an important factor in determinging right and wrong, in deciding what is the will of God. There are great areas of life that are relative but even the relatives of life are informed and guided by the basic absolutes.

While we have said that the individual must determine the will of God for himself, this does not mean that the individual is the final source of authority. The authoritative source is God and his will.

And let us not forget the statement of William Barclay: "There is only one way to bring peace to the heart, joy to the mind, beauty to the life, and that is to accept and to do the will of God." [10] Also, the more central the will of God is in our lives, the more unified we will be. Too many Christians as well as men in general are, as Kierkegaard expressed it, "a colony of incoherent desires and contradictory impulses." The Christian should have one dominant desire: to do the will of God; and one controlling impulse: to glorify God.

How wonderful it would be if all children of God could honestly say with the Psalmist: "I delight to do thy will, O my God" (Ps. 40:8) and could sincerely pray, "Teach me to do they will" (Ps. 143:10). The more fully we let the resurrected Christ live in us, the more we will be able to say as the shadow of a cross looms before us, "Nevertheless, not as I will, but as thou wilt" (Matt. 26:39). May we long for a time when we will "do wholeheartedly the will of God" (Eph. 6:6, NEB).

FOR THOUGHT AND DISCUSSION

1. Can you see the relation of the circumstantial will of

God and/or the lesser-of-two-evils theory to some of our daily decision, such as divorce, remarriage, "telling the truth" to one with terminal illness, "speaking our mind frankly" when asked for an opinion?

2. What is your viewpoint concerning the relation of the will of God to war? Would you ever justify war? Under what conditions? Does Weatherhead's distinction between the intentional and the circumstantial will of God help you?

What about the conscientious objector? What do you think should be the church's attitude? the government's attitude? What about the selective conscientious objector—one who objects to a certain war or a certain type of war? Should his right of conscientious objection be defended by the church? Should the government make provision for him?

3. There has been considerable debate about the legitimacy of dissent. What restrictions, if any, would you place on dissent? Would you ever justify civil disobedience? If so, under what conditions? Would you restrict it to "passive disobedience" or would you ever justify the use of force? What should be the attitude of the dissenter toward the government? What if he is put in prison? Is he ever justified from the Christian perspective in advocating the overthrow of the government?

VIII

Its Supreme Value:
The Kingdom Of God

The child of God, as is true of men in general, needs a unifying center around which he can build his life. It has been said that "all men who attain have one great ruling aim." There may and will be other centers or aims, but these will be subservient to and integrated into the one unifying center or "ruling aim." The more thorough the unification or integration, the more completely the individual will fulfill his potentiality.

There is no aim or center, for the Christian, that is more inclusive or adequate, than his devotion to the kingdom, the rule, the reign of God. This means, among other things, that the supreme value for the Christian is God-centered rather than man-centered. This is in harmony with the distinctly Christian approach to life—God is always the predominant point of reference. In contrast, the philosophical approach is man-centered. For example, the *summum bonum* in philosophical ethics is found within man: it is happiness, wisdom, self-realization, or the greatest happiness of the greatest number.

The Christian discovers that when he puts God, his will, his work, his kingdom first in his life he receives as a by-product the deepest, most abiding and most meaningful happiness and personal fulfillment. He also discovers that as he "seeks first the kingdom of God," he ministers most effectively to the needs of his fellowman. In other words, one who places the kingdom first in his life also in the truest sense puts his fellowman first.

The Meaning of "The Kingdom"[1]

One of the difficulties in any study of the kingdom of God is the fact that it is not clearly defined in the Scriptures. As prominent as the kingdom was in the preaching and teaching of Jesus, he never defined it. He evidently assumed that the people who heard him speak of the kingdom knew what he meant. It is relatively clear that the concept of the kingdom of God was and is closely related to if not an integral part of the idea of the kingship of God. The kingdom describes or represents the relation of God as king to men as subjects. From the perspective of the king, the kingdom signifies his dignity and power. His dignity is something inherently his as king. His power is an external expression of his basic nature and dignity. Both God and men have some distinctive relations to and contributions to make to the kingdom. God, as king, provides guidance and protection. Men as subjects of the king are to trust him and to be loyal and obedient to him. The kingdom can be interpreted either as the reign or the realm of the king. From the biblical perspective, the primary emphasis is on the reign.

The whole kingdom concept is closely related to the idea of the sovereignty of God. When "kingdom" and "sovereignty" are properly understood they can be equated. The king is sovereign. His kingdom represents his sovereignty or rule. This means that for practical purposes the kingdom of God can be equated with the intentional will of God. The prayer

> Thy kingdom come,
> Thy will be done,

On earth as it is in heaven.
(Matt. 6:10)

is not two petitions but one.

Another matter that creates some problems in properly interpreting the meaning of the kingdom of God is the fact that Matthew uses the term kingdom of heaven. This term or expression is found thirty-one times in Matthew, with only three references to the Kingdom of God (19:24; 21:31, 43). In contrast, Mark and Luke speak of the Kingdom of God sixteen and thirty-two times, respectively, and do not use the phrase "kingdom of heaven" at all.[2] It seems relatively clear that the two phrases can be equated (see Matt. 19:23, 24). This is particularly evident when one compares parallel verses in Matthew, Mark, and Luke (Matt. 19:23; Mark 10:23; and Luke 18:24).

What is the reason for the difference in Matthew and the other synoptics? The usual explanation and evidently the correct one is that devout Jews so reverenced the name of God that they sought to avoid using his name. Matthew was the most Jewish of the gospel writers and seemingly wrote his gospel primarily for Jewish readers. Hence he avoided the use of "kingdom of God" and substituted "kingdom of heaven."

In addition to "kingdom of God" and "kingdom of heaven," there are a number of biblical references to "the kingdom of the Father" (see Matt. 13:43; 26:29; cf. Matt. 25:34; Luke 12:32). Also the word "kingdom" is frequently used in an absolute sense without any defining word or phrase but where the reference is clearly to the . "kingdom of God."

Jesus and the Kingdom

When Jesus came, saying, "The kingdom of God is at hand" (Mark 1:15), he was using a familiar term. The Jews in the days of Jesus connected the kingdom idea with messianic hopes, which flourished among them.[3] The idea of the kingship of God is very prevalent in the Old Testament. In the earlier days the kingship concept was restricted, in the main, to Israel. As the nation declined, the remnant idea became more prevalent and God tended, in a sense, to be the king only of those who voluntarily accepted his reign. There is also found in the Old Testament the idea that the Lord will "reign for ever and ever" (Ex. 15:18) and that his kingship is universal. He was recognized as "king of all the earth" (Ps. 47:7), as a God who "reigns over the nations" (Ps. 47:8).

The Jews in the days of Jesus looked forward to the coming of the kingdom of God as a time when God's judgment would come upon their enemies and as a time of national justification, restoration, and exaltation. They also thought of it as an earthly kingdom to be set up and ruled over by the Messiah or the Son of Man.

As was so frequently true, Jesus utilized current terminology but breathed new life and meaning into the old. He definitely rejected the idea of an earthly kingdom with the Messiah as the king of the kingdom. He largely ignored the nationalistic elements of the current Jewish perspective. He did not abolish entirely the idea of the kingdom as a future hope, but he also made it a present reality. As John Bright says, "The future tense of the Old Testament. . .has now become an emphatic present. . . .In the person and work of Jesus the Kingdom of God has intruded into the world."[4] This does not necessarily mean that the sense of the future was discarded. Pannenberg, whose major emphasis is on the "imminent kingdom" (it "was the resounding motif of Jesus' message"), suggests that "it is a mark of Jesus' proclamation of the Kingdom of God that future and present are inextricably interwoven." He further says, "Jesus underscored the present impact of the imminent future."[5] He also suggests that the main way Jesus modified the Jewish conception of the kingdom was his emphasis on its imminence.

There can be no question about the centrality of the kingdom of God in the ministry of Jesus. It was the subject of his earliest recorded preaching: "the kingdom of God is at hand" (Mark 1:15; cf. Matt. 4:17), was his continuing theme, and when he appeared to the disciples after his resurrection he spoke to them concerning the kingdom of God (Acts 1:3). The idea of the kingdom permeated and dominated his entire ministry. It was the key or unifying theme of his preaching and teaching. For example, almost all of his parables were kingdom parables. L. H. Marshall suggests that *"all the ethical teaching of Jesus is simply an exposition of the ethics of the Kingdom of God, of the way in which men inevitably behave when they actually come under the rule of God."*[6]

Since the kingdom was central in the life and ministry of Jesus, it was natural and inevitable that it would be central in his instructions to his disciples. It was the first specific petition in the prayer he taught his disciples to pray (Matt. 6:10). This implies that before a disciple of Christ has any right to pray, "Give us this day our daily bread," "forgive us our debts," or "lead us not into temptation" he must pray, "Thy kingdom come." This is not the prayer of a pious person who wants to escape from the world or of a reformer who thinks he can remake the world. Rather, it is the prayer of the child of God who lives in the world, and who recognizes that the kingdom is God's and that he alone can bring it to realization in the world.

Jesus also instructed his disciples and would instruct us to seek first the kingdom of God and his righteousness (Matt. 6:33). This should be accompanied with a childlike trust that the heavenly Father knows our needs and will provide the necessities of life for us. James Hastings suggests that "seek first his kingdom" is Jesus' definition of the chief good. Jesus also compared the kingdom to the "treasure hidden in a field" and to a "pearl of great value." When one discovered the hidden treasure or the pearl of great value he "went and sold all that he had and bought it" (Matt. 13:44–46). The kingdom is the supreme value for the child of God.

The kingdom was of central importance in the continuing ministry of the disciples. When Jesus sent out the twelve, they were instructed to preach as they went, saying, "The kingdom of heaven is at hand" (Matt. 10:7, cf. Luke 9:2). Similarly, the seventy, when they were sent out on a missionary journey, were to preach "The kingdom of God has come near to you" (Luke 10:9).

The Nature of the Kingdom

Let us examine in more detail the nature of the kingdom, basing our study primarily on the teachings of Jesus. Where else could we go for an authoritative word concerning the nature of the kingdom? Unfortunately, some biblical scholars attempt to press everything Jesus said concerning the kingdom into their pre-conceived concept or mold. Isolated verses can be quoted to support widely divergent interpretations. However, all that Jesus taught concerning the kingdom cannot be wrapped into one neat little package. His teachings contain varying and at least on the surface paradoxical perspectives.

It will help us properly to interpret and evaluate these seeming paradoxes if we will keep in mind that the kingdom is basically spiritual and inner. Paul says that "the kingdom of God does not mean food and drink but righteousness and peace and joy in the Holy Spirit" (Rom. 14:17). But while basically it is a spiritual kingdom there is also a deep and an abiding concern for the material well-being of people. In the model prayer immediately following the prayer for the kingdom is the petition for daily bread (Matt. 6:10, 11). The basis of the separation of the sheep and the goats at the time of judgment was their service to the hungry, thirsty, lonely, naked, sick, and imprisoned (Matt. 25:3, 5–36, 42–43). The main contrast regarding the kingdom is not between the spiritual and the material but between the spiritual and the physical. Since the kingdom is basically spiritual and inner, it should not and cannot be identified with any earthly, man-made structure or organization, not even the church. This spiritual kingdom is naturally and inevitably primarily inner. But just as inevitably it has its outer manifestations.

Also, the kingdom is a gift of God: "It is your Father's good pleasure to give you the kingdom" (Luke 12:32). As a gift it is to be received (Mark 10:15). It is also to be prayed for (Matt. 6:10), and what we pray for we should work for. We can even say that when we experience it as a gift we accept it as a task. In this regard, the Kingdom is somewhat comparable to the Promised Land, which was given to Israel by the Lord, and yet they had to struggle to win it.

One of the most prevalent and perplexing paradoxes concerning the kingdom is that it is a present reality and yet a future hope. Barth expresses something of this idea when he says that according to the Old and New Testaments the rule or government of God "is always a completed fact. . .which can be known to us, and yet also an imminent event towards which we are only moving and which is still concealed from us."[7] The present and the future aspects of the kingdom were not really antithetical in the life and activity of Jesus. The kingdom as future was evident in the teachings of Jesus but it was a future that had already broken into the present. The imminent kingdom had become the invading kingdom, being present in the world in the life and ministry of the Messiah, the Son of God. "The kingdom of God is the lordship of God established in the world in Jesus Christ. It is the rule of God as it takes place in Him."⁸ There is also a very real sense in which the kingdom is timeless just as God is timeless. He is the great "I am." Christ is "the Alpha and the Omega. . .who is and who was and who is to come" (Rev. 1:8). The timelessness of the kingdom is comparable to the dynamic nature of the Christian life. We are saved in all tenses. We have been saved, are in the process of being saved, and shall be saved. The kingdom has come, is a present reality, and yet it is a future hope. The present ties the past and future together.

The culmination or consummation of the kingdom may come soon or late, sudden or gradual, but it must and will come. Jesus plainly taught that no one knew when it would come. His main emphasis was that the disciple was to watch and be ready at any time. Jesus did teach that the kingdom was imminent (see Mark 1:15). This note was also present in the writings of Paul: "the appointed time has grown very short" (1 Cor. 7:29; cf. Rom. 13:11–12); in Hebrews: "you see the Day drawing near" (Heb. 10:29); in James: "establish your hearts, for the coming of the Lord is at hand" (James 5:8); in Peter: "the end of all things is at hand" (1 Peter 4:7); in John: "children, it is the last hour" (1 John 2:18); and in Revelation: "the time is near" (Rev. 1:3; cf. 22:7–7, 20). Some biblical scholars contend that all of these were wrong about the imminence of the coming of the kingdom. Is there not a possibility that this is the correct and the healthiest attitude for any one to have regarding the consummation of the kingdom? It can be considered as always imminent though its consummation may be long delayed. At least a consciousness that it may come in its fullness at any time will encourage us to be alert, to seek to be ready for its coming.

An examination of some of the scriptures mentioned above as well as other references will reveal that the eschatological and ethical aspects of the kingdom do not stand out in marked contrast. Neither dominates the other. Some scholars seek to unlock every door of the kingdom with the eschatological key but that key does not fit every door. The teachings of Jesus are largely but not exclusively set in an eschatological framework. Really, the eschatological aspects of his teachings are closely related to his ethics. The two—eschatology and ethics—belong together, although all of his ethical teachings are not eschatological in perspective. There is a close relation of eschatology and ethics not only in the teachings of Jesus' but also in other portions of the New Testament. For example, the imminence of the coming kingdom is used at times as the basis for ethical exhortations. An example is the above reference to First Peter. His statement "The end of all things is at hand" is followed with "therefore keep sane and sober for your prayers. Above all hold unfailing your love for one another. . . . Practice hospitality. . . . As each has received a gift, employ it for one another" (1 Pet. 4:7–10). The general relation of eschatology and ethics is clearly evident in Paul's great chapter on the resurrection. At the close of the chapter he breaks out in those often quoted words:

> "Death is swallowed up in victory."
> "O death, where is thy victory?
> O death, where is thy sting?"
> The sting of death is sin, and the
> power of sin is the law. But thanks be
> to God, who gives us the victory
> through our Lord Jesus Christ.

Then notice the exhortation that follows immediately:

> Therefore, my beloved brethren, be
> steadfast, immovable, always abounding
> in the work of the Lord, knowing
> that in the Lord your labor is not in vain.
>
> (1 Cor. 15:54–58)

Citizens of the Kingdom

Since the kingdom is the supreme value for the Christian, it is important that we understand the conditions for entrance into and the grounds for greatness in the kingdom, along with the ways that we can help to promote the kingdom among men.

One problem about discussing "entrance into the kingdom" is that many people find it difficult to understand how one can enter a spiritual kingdom. They associate "entrance" with a door or a gate, with something physical and material. But when a child of God submits to the rule or reign of God he enters the kingdom of God. There is a sense in which this is a one-time entrance. But since our submission to the rule, reign, or will of God is never perfect, our entrance into the kingdom in another sense is never complete; it is a continous process. We have entered but we are also entering.

What are the conditions for entrance? There are several plainly stated by Jesus. (1) Repentance: "The kingdom of God is at hand; repent, and believe in the gospel" (Mark 1:15). (2) Childlikeness: "Whoever does not receive the kingdom of God like a child shall not enter it" (Mark 10:15; cf. Matt. 18:3; 19:14; Luke 18:16–17). (3) Obedience: "Not every one who says to me, 'Lord, Lord,' shall enter the kingdom of heaven, but he who does the will of my Father who is in heaven" (Matt. 7:21). (4) Righteousness: "Unless your righteousness exceeds that of the scribes and Pharisees, you will never enter the kingdom of heaven" (Matt. 5:20). (5) Unselfish unconscious service to those in need: the hungry, the thirsty, the stranger, the naked, the sick, the imprisoned (Matt. 25:31–46). These ministries, however, may be as much an evidence that one is in the kingdom as they are requirements for entrance into the kingdom.

"There is at least one other major condition for entrance into the kingdom. It is single-minded devotion to the kingdom and the things of God." This is where the rich young ruler failed. To enter the kingdom "one must be willing to give up anything that stands between himself and supreme devotion to the Kingdom of God. This emphasis on single-minded devotion is the background for the hyperbolic statement by Jesus to cut off, if necessary, a hand or a foot, or to pluck out an eye. He said, 'It is better for you to enter the kingdom of God with one eye than with two eyes to be thrown into hell' (Mark 9:47; Matt. 18:9). The Kingdom is worth any sacrifice; it is life's supreme value."[10]

The beatitudes, standing at the beginning of the so-called Sermon on the Mount, mention qualities that indicate that one is in the kingdom. The relation to the kingdom is spelled out specifically in the first beatitude: "Blessed are the poor in spirit, for theirs is the kingdom of heaven" (Matt. 5:3; cf. Luke 6:20). Exactly the same ending is found in the last of the beatitudes, or next to last if verse 11 and 12 are considered separate beatitudes. The statement is: "Blessed are those who are persecuted for righteousness' sake, for theirs is the kingdom of heaven" (Matt. 5:10).

The subject of greatness in the kingdom was evidently a relatively frequent topic of conversation among the disciples. On at least one occasion they pointedly asked Jesus, "Who is the greatest in the kingdom of heaven?" (Matt. 18:1). He called a child and placing him in the midst of them said, "Whoever humbles himself like this child, he is the greatest in the kingdom of heaven" (Matt. 18:4). On another occasion John and James (Mark 10:35), with their mother (Matt. 20:20), requested the chief seats in Christ's kingdom. Jesus reminded them and the other disciples that worldly rulers lorded it over the people. This was not to be true in his kingdom. He said, "Whoever would be great among you must be your servant; and whoever would be first among you must be slave of all" (Mark 10:43–44; Matt. 20:26–27). In this area as always, he exemplified in his own life what he expected of his followers: "For the Son of Man also came not to be served but to serve, and to give his life as a ransom for many" (Mark 10:45; Matt. 20:28).

What are our responsibilities regarding the kingdom? Most of these have been mentioned. We should pray for its coming, recognizing that it comes as God's will is done on earth as it is in heaven. We should be supremely devoted to the kingdom. It should be, in practice as well as in theory, the supreme value in our personal lives. We should seek the kingdom first, valuing it above all worldly and material things. We should be willing to make any sacrifice for the sake of the kingdom: material possessions, family ties, even life itself. Loyalty to the kingdom of God and to the God of the kingdom should come first in our lives.

We extend the kingdom of God as we increasingly open our hearts and lives to the rule or reign of God. We promote his kingdom as we extend his righteous reign not only in our own lives but also in the lives of others and in the society in which we live. Let us be careful, however, that we do not get an exalted conception of our contribution to the kingdom. Let us never forget that it is *his* kingdom. He gives it although there may be some activity even in accepting a gift. And, as suggested earlier, a promised land that is given must be won. The kingdom is God's supreme gift and man's supreme task. When we think about the uncertainty of the consummation of the kingdom, the supreme admonition is to watch, to be on the alert. This means that we should "sit loose" not only to things temporal but also to our own lives.

Inclusiveness of the Kingdom

The kingdom of God is or should be the supreme value not only for the individual but also for the home, the local church, the denomination, the nation, and the world. Just as surely as God is the sovereign God of the universe his rule, reign, or kingdom is to be inclusive of the totality of the lives of the peoples of the world and of all their institutions and agencies. The ultimate and inclusive purpose of all institutions is to increase or spread God's kingdom of love and righteousness.

While all peoples and all institutions are finally responsible to the sovereign God, Christians and Christian institutions are related to and responsible to God the king and his kingdom in a unique way. Unfortunately, many Christians attempt to serve both the kingdom of God and the kingdom of the world. They have forgotten that Jesus said, "You *cannot* serve God and mammon"; he did not say, "You *should not* serve God and mammon." Someone has suggested that we should not be an amphibian, half in one world and half in the other. An attempt to be an amphibian assures us not only of an ineffective life for the Lord but also of a miserable existence. A major fault of many of us as Christians is not that we are particularly bad, but that we live for the "good" rather than the "best" and of course the best is the kingdom of God.

Christian institutions such as the home and the church are not ends within themselves. They serve or should serve the purposes of the kingdom. What a contribution would be made to the cause of Christ if Christian young people entering marriage realized that their newly-established home was to be an instrument for the extension of the rule or kingdom of God! They would also discover that such a perspective would eliminate or solve most of the potential problems they might have.

Particularly important for our study is the relation of the church and the kingdom. It is wise to remember in the beginning that the two cannot be equated. Furthermore, the church should not be considered the present form of the kingdom. Membership in one does not necessarily mean membership in the other. Citizenship in the kingdom is spiritual membership. Membership in a church should not be, but may be, merely formal and external. The kingdom is more inclusive than the church. It is beyond the church—beyond in two directions—past and future. However, as and to the degree that the church recognizes the kingdom as something beyond the church, the kingdom will manifest itself in and through the church. The church is a product of the kingdom, moves or should move toward the kingdom, and should be an instrument of the kingdom. As Pannenburg suggests, "the central concern of the Church, and the primary point of reference for understanding the Church, must be the Kingdom of God."[11] It is even possible for the institutional church to be an enemy of the kingdom. Since God cannot be ultimately defeated in his purposes in and for the world, he may turn to so-called secular forces and organizations as the primary agencies for the promotion of his kingdom. One reason for the word "primary" in the preceding sentence is the continuing evidence that God uses all men and all institutions and organizations to varying degrees to extend his righteous rule in the world. This is even true of those who oppose him.

The sovereign God holds nations as well as individuals, homes, and churches, responsible. Nations are to be subservient to and serve the purposes of the kingdom of God. In so far as they fail to do this the judgment of God will come upon them.

In other words, what we have been suggesting is that the kingdom of our sovereign God embraces the totality of the life of the world. We should remember, however, that since the kingdom is eternal and spiritual it can never be fully contained in and expressed through any human organization or institution. This means, among other things, that the kingdom should never be equated with the *status quo* or with any program to change the *status quo*. The kingdom can never be completely realized within history unless we include eternity as a part of history. On the other hand, the kingdom is the most dynamic force in the historic process. While the Christian believes that the fulfillment of the kingdom "is bound to eternity and no imagination can reach the eternal," yet he also believes that "fragmentary anticipations" of the kingdom are possible in the here and now.[12]

FOR THOUGHT AND DISCUSSION

1. What are some things that our churches could do that would enable them to contribute more to the promotion of the kingdom of God? What about the basis on which they judge their success? Where should be or where is the primary emphasis: on people or on programs and structures? How much and in what ways do you think the materialistic spirit of the contemporary world has affected our churches? In turn, how does this affect the contribution of the church to the kingdom?

2. Should the church as such get involved in doing anything about the problems of society, such as alcoholism, crime, drug abuse, poverty? Or should it depend exclusively on the work of members of the church, restricting itself to inspiring them to apply the gospel to the problems that they and their society face? In other words, should the church's involvement in the problems of society be direct, indirect, or both direct and indirect?

3. How far do you think the government can and should

go in limiting the publication and distribution of pornographic materials? Is any restriction a violation of "the freedom of speech" guaranteed by the first amendment to the U. S. Constitution?

IX

Its Comprehensive Ideal: Perfection

The word "comprehensive" in the heading of this chapter correctly implies that there are other significant ideals for the Christian life. Some of those ideals have been discussed in preceding chapters, others will be considered in succeeding chapters. Some are closely related to, if not an integral part of, perfection. For example, the intentional will of God (Chap. VII) is expressive of or can be equated with perfection. The same can be said of any full or undiluted expression of *agape* or gift-love in contrast to a need-love (Chap. X). The kingdom, (Chap. VIII) when it fully comes, means perfection.

Just as God's intentional will never finds complete expression even in the lives of God's best people, and just as the kingdom will never come fully until God's appointed time for its culmination, and just as *agape* or gift-love never finds undiluted expression outside of God, so perfection as an ideal for the individual Christian and for society is never fully attained in this life.

None of the preceding concepts or ideals, however, is nullified, abrogated, or made irrelevant by its unattainability. It is their unattainability that actually makes these ideals abidingly relevant. They continue to challenge men and the society of men to the end of life. If any of them could be attained, they would then cease to challenge and in a very real sense lose their relevance. The preceding and other basic expectations of our Christian faith will not be fully attained or expressed in our lives until we awake at the end of life in his likeness. It is then that we shall be known as we are known. We shall "understand fully" (1 Cor. 13:12). So it is with every aspect of the Christian life. At best it is now partial or incomplete and will remain so throughout life. But there will come a time when the partial will give way to the whole, the incomplete to the complete, the imperfect to the perfect.

The Meaning of Perfection

We can derive some insight into the meaning of perfection by an understanding of the words translated "perfect" and "perfection" and by the varied translations of those words. The main words in the Old Testament are *shalem* and closely related *tam* and *tamim*. While the first of these words is frequently translated "perfect" in the King James Version, it is usually translated "whole" or "wholly true" in the Revised Standard Version, and in a few places, "blameless." *Shalem* is particularly prevalent in the books of Kings and Chronicles. It frequently refers to a "whole," "wholly true," or perfect heart (see 1 Kings 8:61; 15:3, 14; 2 Kings 20:3; 1 Chron. 28:9; 29:9, 19; 2 Chron. 19:4).

Tam is translated "blameless" or "blameless and upright" in the Revised Standard Version in contrast to "perfect" in the King James Version (see Job 1:1, 8; 2:3; 8:20; 9:20, 21, 22; Ps. 64:4). On the other hand, *tamim* is rather frequently translated "perfect" in the Revised Standard Version. A few such references are: "the way of the Lord is perfect" (2 Sam. 22:31; Ps. 18:30), the knowledge of the Lord is perfect (Job 37:16; 36:4), and "the law of the Lord is perfect" (Ps. 19:7). When applied to the animals that were used for sacrificial purposes *tamim* is usually translated "without blemish," with forty to fifty such references.

An animal without blemish would be perfect as far as the requirements for the sacrifices.

In the New Testament there is also more than one word translated "perfect." In the vast majority of cases, however, the word is *teleios* or *teleioo*. The basic meaning is "end" or "complete."

The Revised Standard Version translates *teleios* or *teleioo* "mature" in several places: "among the mature we do impart wisdom" (1 Cor. 2:6); "let those of us who are mature ["spiritually mature," TEV] be thus minded" (Phil. 3:15); "that we may present every man mature in Christ" (Col. 1:28); "that you may stand mature" (Col. 4:12). In Ephesians, Paul speaks of the "equipment" ["perfecting," KJV] of the saints (Eph. 4:12), while James says that "faith was completed by works" (Jas. 2:22).

But *teleios* and *teleioo* are most frequently translated, even in the Revised Standard Version, "perfect." Jesus said to his disciples, "You, therefore, must be perfect" (Matt. 5:48), and to the rich young ruler, "If you would be perfect" ["if you wish to go the whole way," NEB] (Matt. 19:21). Paul refers to the "good and acceptable and perfect" will of God (Rom. 12:2) and to the power of God that "is made perfect ["comes to full strength," NEB] in weakness" (2 Cor. 12:9). The author of Hebrews says that Christ was made "perfect through suffering" (Heb. 2:10) and "that being made perfect he became the source of eternal salvation to all who obey him" (Heb. 5:9). James speaks of a "perfect gift" (Jas. 1:17), "the perfect law" (Jas. 1:25), and "a perfect man" (Jas. 3:2). John says that God's love "is perfected in us" (1 John 4:12) and that "perfect love casteth out ["banishes," NEB] fear" (1 John 4:18).

The preceding word study suggests several synonyms for "perfection" that help to define it and to reveal something of its comprehensiveness. To be perfect means to be whole, sound, true, blameless, unblemished, complete, mature, full-grown. For example, when Paul refers to the will of God as perfect (*teleion*) it could mean "blameless" or "unblemished" or on the other hand it could mean "complete" or "whole." When Paul says that "love binds everything together in perfect harmony" (Col. 3:14), it could be translated "in complete harmony."

The idea of perfection in the Bible goes far beyond the use of particular words. The invitation or instruction, so common in the Old Testament, to walk in the way of the Lord refers to a way of perfection. The invitation of Jesus, "Come, follow me," is not exclusively an initial invitation to a physical journey but also a recurring and continuing invitation to his way in human and divine relations. As such it is an invitation to a way of perfection. Thielicke says, "The commandments of God are uncompromising in their demands,"[1] and hence set forth an ideal of perfection. Similarly, the basic teachings of Jesus are stated in terms of perfection: a love that lays down its life (John 15:13), forgiveness until seventy times seven (Matt. 18:22).

Perfection, as set forth in the Scriptures, is all-inclusive. It applies to the individual child of God but also to the society of men. When we consider the strictly individual or personal aspects of perfection, which will be our concern through the remainder of this chapter, it becomes clear that Christian perfection is very comprehensive. For example, it has both negative and positive aspects. This, in turn, means that perfection involves more than sinlessness unless sin is interpreted in broad terms. An adequate conception of sin would include both sins of omission and commission. Also, sin would have to be interpreted as inner as well as outer.

Although John Wesley is not entirely clear concerning his definition of perfection, his emphasis is on inner motives and purposes. For example, Christian perfection for him is "that love of God and neighbour which implies deliverance from *all sin*"[2] While Christian perfection may be more concerned with motives and inner attitudes than with outer conduct, it is and should be concerned with both. And after all, what one is inwardly he will become outwardly. This is so inevitably true that one can judge, to a large degree, what is on the inside by what is expressed outwardly. And actually, who would claim that he is perfect inwardly, that his motives are always pure, that he loves God supremely and his neighbor as himself?

The preceding implies that a distinction should be made between relative and absolute perfection. "Relative" perfection on the surface is contradictory. It is hard, however, to avoid the recognition and use of some such word. Wesley suggested that there was a sense in which there was no absolute perfection on earth. He said that there was no perfection "which does not admit of a continual increase."[3] The idea of a relative perfection should not surprise us. The Christian life in general is portrayed over and over again in some closely related and meaningful paradoxes. When we came into union with Christ the marred image of God was restored within us and yet it is in the process of being restored.

We may be mature in the faith, and yet we are in the process of maturing. Just as a baby may be considered a perfect physical specimen yet be immature, so a babe in Christ may possess some degree of perfection, a perfection that belongs to the immature, but still be very imperfect when measured in terms of full maturity. There continues to be growth or movement in his life. Paul plainly said of himself, "I have not yet reached perfection," but notice what he added: "but I press on, hoping to take hold of that for which Christ once took hold of me" (Phil. 3:12, NEB). As Flew suggests, "Paul's doctrine of perfection is essentially a doctrine of growth."[4] It should possibly be added that no upper limit should be set for that growth. None of us has begun to attain to the degree of maturity or perfection that is a possible attainment for us. Let us emphasize again, however, that whatever degree of perfection we may reach will always be relative, partial, or incomplete. This means, among other things, that Christian perfection is never static; it is always dynamic or growing.

The Measure of Perfection

The dynamic nature of Christian perfection stands out in a particularly prominent and graphic way when we understand that the norm or standard of Christian perfection is God himself. The biblical idea of perfection, in Old Testament and in New Testament, was not derived from a study of the lives of God's great and good men but from the essential nature of God. Christian perfection is not grounded in the nature of the moral law but in the moral nature of the Lawgiver. The ultimate ideal for the Christian is not so much complete obedience to the will of God as it is complete conformity to the nature and character of God. Also, such conformity must first be inner before it can be outwardly effective. This inner conformity will be the highest expression of the will of God and will naturally and inevitably move us toward full obedience to that will.

Nowhere is the ideal of perfection stated more specifically and pointedly than in the words of Jesus to his disciples: "You, therefore, must be perfect (*teleioi*), as your heavenly Father is perfect (*teleios*)" (Matt. 5:48). This is the key verse to an understanding of Christian perfection. It has been called the "perfect precept of Christianity." From the ethical perspective, it is equal in importance to the commandments to love God supremely and one's neighbor as one's self. It, as is true of them, compresses into one statement the teachings of both the Law and the Prophets. The highest ideal, set forth in both Old and New Testaments, is that the child of God is to be like the One he professes to love, worship, and serve (cf. Luke 6:36).

Men through the centuries have sought, in various ways, to tone down the sharpness of the challenge or command by Jesus in Matthew 5:48. It has been suggested, and correctly so, that *teleios* could be translated "blameless," "complete," or "mature." But would a change in translation basically alter the statement? No, the challenge of the statement stems primarily from the words "as your heavenly Father." What difference would it make if we were to translate the statement as follows: "You, therefore, must be complete, mature, or blameless, as your heavenly Father is complete, mature, or blameless"? Whatever term or word is used to describe God, it actually means perfection. The perfection found in God will never be our complete achievement in this life, but it should be the norm or standard by which we judge our lives. It should also be our continuing aspiration, although that aspiration will be and possibly should be more subconscious than conscious.

There is more than one key word in the statement by Jesus. The word "you" is emphatic. This implies that this word is addressed to the disciples and not to those outside the Christian fellowship. It is only those who know God as heavenly Father, those who have been brought into the spiritual family of God, who are challenged to be like him. The child is to be like the Father. This means that "Father" is also a key word in this verse as it is in the Sermon on the Mount in general and in the New Testament as a whole, particularly in Matthew and John. Another key word is "therefore," which is also a key word in many other places in the Bible.

Here the "therefore" simply summarizes what has preceded. It may refer only to verses 43—47, where Jesus had challenged his disciples to be like their Father in their generous treatment of their enemies as well as their friends. However, the "therefore" could refer all the way back to verse 21. At least a child of God will be coming close to the perfection found in God: if he is never angry with his brother (v. 22), never commits psychological adultery by looking at a woman lustfully (v. 28), not only never swears falsely (v. 33) but whose simple "yes" and "no" are sufficient (v. 37), does not practice the *lex talionis*, the law of retaliation (vv. 38–42), and not only loves his neighbor but also his enemy and prays for those who persecute him (vv. 43–44). While that may be the extent of the reference of "therefore," Flew suggests that "the aspiration after perfection gives unity and harmony to the whole discourse [the Sermon on the Mount]." As such he says that it is "like some phrase of music which summarizes and concludes a symphony."[5]

The divine likeness or image which was man's in his original creation and which was marred by sin can be restored through his union with Christ. As suggested previously, this restoration is never complete. We can correctly speak of the divine likeness or image as both a gift and a task. The divine image is not only that from which we have come, it is also that to which we go. As gift it is indicative; as task it is an imperative.[6] And let us never forget that any place and any time when God is injected into the picture it means perfection. And God-perfection, from the human perspective, is always open-ended and indefinite, never definte and final.

In regard to God-likeness, as well as elsewhere, Jesus set the example. He came into the world not to do his own will but the will of the Father. He had a sense of holy urgency as he went about the Father's work. He said, "The Son can do nothing of his own accord, but only what he sees the Father doing" (John 5:19). What was true of him should be true of us. In the highest and deepest sense we are to be imitators of him. It was Paul who said, "Be imitators of me as I am of Christ" (1 Cor. 11:1) and who appealed to the Thessalonians, "And you became imitators of us and of the Lord" (1 Thess. 1:6). Here is the measure of perfection and also of every other aspect of the Christian life. "The best Christian living has always been in some sort an imitation of Christ; not a slavish copying of His acts but the working of His mind and spirit into new contexts of life and circumstances."[7] Or, as Tinsley says concerning Paul, "The *imitatio Christi.* . .was not the attempt to copy a wholly external object;. . .it was an active dynamic process, initiated, sustained and directed by the Spirit, involving a mutual personal and reciprocal relationship."[8]

This is the measure of perfection for the Christian and for the Christian life in general. Jesus himself said, "It is enough for the disciple to be like his teacher, and the servant like his master" (Matt. 10:25). Again he said, "A disciple is not above his teacher, but every one when he is fully taught ["is perfect," KJV] will be like his teacher" (Luke 6:40). Peter said, "As he who called you is holy, be holy yourselves in all your conduct" (1 Pet. 1:15), while John wrote, "He who says he abides in him ought to walk in the same way in which he walked" (1 John 2:6). For Paul the Christian life was "preeminently 'walking' in the 'Way of Christ.' "[9] The ultimate ideal is "a mature manhood" or "a perfect measure of Christ's moral stature" (Eph. 4:13, Wm.). How do we measure up when we compare ourselves to the moral stature of Christ? When we stand in the presence of the Perfect One, do we not feel like crying out as Isaiah did, "Woe is me! For I am lost; for I am a man of unclean lips"? Why the cry? "For my eyes have seen the King, the Lord of Hosts!" (Isa. 6.5).

The Means of Perfection

What is our hope for some movement toward the wholeness, the perfection found in God? How should we react when we realize that such perfection is an ideal or a dream beyound our attainment? Should we rationalize our sins and failures and be satisfied to live on a level far below the ideal? Or, should we constantly judge our present level of living by the ideal of perfection and feel the consequent and constant tug of heart to move toward the high or upward call of God in Christ Jesus, which is a call to perfection?

The answers to the preceding questions are self-evident. Any Christian who is serious about living the Christian life knows that he must never lose that inner tug, the constant tension between the level on which he is now living and the level toward which he knows he should move. One thing that should encourage the Christian is the assurance that his heavenly Father understands his weaknesses and limitations, will forgive his sins and failures, and if he will repent he will restore him to full fellowship.

What can we do to move ourselves toward the full maturity or perfection that is God's ultimate ideal for our lives and in that way relieve some of the tension created by our imperfection? Really, can we do anything? Are there any means available that will help us move in the right direction? Still another question: How much conscious effort should be made to attain the unattainable?

It does seem that some conscious effort on our part is justified and wise. At least we can meet some of the conditions that are necesary for any progress toward perfection or Christian maturity. For example, faith is just as essential for such progress or movement as it was at the beginning of the Christian life. There is also an important place for the cultivation of one's inner spiritual life through meditation, prayer, and Bible reading and study. Furthermore, the readiness with which we respond to the touch of the Divine Spirit on our spirits will determine, to a considerable degree, the direction in which our lives will move. As implied earlier, there needs to be an important place in our lives for genuine repentance not only for our overt sins but also for inner and sometimes hidden sins of motive, purpose, idea, and ideal.

There are some dangers in seeking deliberately and consciously our own perfection. If such a search becomes a prominent feature of our lives it will tend to make us unhealthily introspective. We will tend to become too self-centered. Really, any movement toward perfection in our lives will come primarily as a by-product of the cultivation of our inner relations to our Lord and of service to our fellowman in his name.

Most of the preceding will apply to the imitation of Christ, which is a prominent aspect of the Christian life. How much should we seek consciously to imitate Christ, who lived a perfect life? Any conscious effort at imitation would tend to be primarily if not exclusively external in results. What is needed far more is a reproduction in our lives of his spirit accompanied by motives and purposes akin to his. Such inner conformity occurs only in association with him. It is the product of the mysterious hidden work of the Divine Spirit within our lives. There is a very real sense in which Christ is not only the object of the imitation but also the means for its achievement. He is not only the end or goal of the Christian journey, he is also the guide and companion on the journey, and in the final analysis he is the journey, the road, and the way. Our association with him on the journey is our main hope for movement toward the maturity, wholeness, or perfection found in him.

This movement stems more or less naturally from the nature of the Christian experience. When we became children of God, we were brought into a vital life-changing union with the resurrected Christ. He is in us, and we are in him. As Forsyth once said, "growth is progress, not to Christ but in Christ." We begin as babes in Christ but the vitality of the relation to Christ is the secret to growth and movement toward perfection. The most important thing we can do is to open our lives more fully to the indwelling Christ, permitting him to live in us and to express himself more completely through us.

Paul said that the Colossians had "put on the new nature" but notice what is added: "which is being renewed in knowledge after the image of its creator" (Col. 3:10). Here is achievement and process. To the Ephesians he wrote: "We are to grow up in every way into him who is the head, unto Chirst" (Eph. 4:15). We are "in Christ," yet we are to grow up "into him." It is through our union and continuing assocation with our risen Lord that we "are being changed into his likeness from one degree of glory to another" (2 Cor. 3:18). Notice that the verb is passive: "are being changed." We do not change ourselves. We are changed. The process as well as the original experience is of grace. As Pascal says, "grace is indeed needed to turn a man into a saint; and he who doubts it does not know what a saint or a man is." We do believe that "he who began a good work" in us "will bring it to completion at the day of Jesus Christ" (Phil. 1:6).

Conclusions Concerning Perfection

There are some dangers that need to be guarded against when perfection is made the ultimate ideal of the Christian life. One is the tendency to identify perfection with sinlessness. The danger is particularly prevalent when there is a limited or restricted view of sin, considering it entirely a matter of inner motives or interpreting it largely or exclusively in negative terms. One is considered perfect if he does not _____ and_____ and _____. Some with the latter view of sin claim or believe that they have attained "sinless perfection." Such persons are tempted to be excessively self-centered, to become self-satisfied, to develop a pharisaical "holier-than-thou attitude," to be afflicted with an overdose of spiritual pride, and to be harshly critical of those who are not "perfect." In the main, they have lost the drive so essential in creative Christian living.

There are some dangers even to those who make a distinction between relative and absolute perfection, who interpret sin in its most inclusive terms, and who consider perfection a gradual achievement. Such a person may get discouraged. He may feel that even relative perfection is beyond his grasp. He may be beset with the insidious temptation to settle down to a mediocre type of Christian life rather than to feel the constant and disturbing tug to come up higher.

Also, many who accept perfection as an ideal tend to become absolutists. They see everything as right or wrong, black or white. For them there is no gray area. The lesser-of-two-evils theory when applied to the decisions of Christians represents for them a defeating compromise. We will admit that there are dangers in the lesser-of-two-evils theory, but something comparable to it is necessary for a Christian motivated by an ideal of perfection who lives in a very imperfect world.

We admit that there are dangers in accepting or making perfection the ultimate Christian idea, but there are greater dangers for the Christian if he accepts anything less than perfection as the ultimate ideal. Entirely too many Christians have become immune to the full meaning of the Christian life by being innoculated with its diluted form which is so prevalent among us.

In contrast to the preceding, there are three or four positive and very meaningful contributions that the ideal of perfection can and will make to the Christian's life. As suggested previously, perfection, when properly interpreted, will make our Christian faith abidingly relevant. Such perfection represents what Reinhold Niebuhr has referred to as "the relevance of an impossible ethical ideal." It is not relevant in spite of its impossibility; it is abidingly relevant because of its impossibility.

The ideal of perfection points up and underscores our imperfections. They tend to stand out in bold relief. Because of our evident imperfections, we continue to need the warning restrictive influence of the law. Thielicke suggests that the law is a "kind of sheep dog whose purpose is to recall the members of the flock to the path,"[10] a path that moves us toward the ultimate goal of our lives: perfection.

Another comparable contribution of perfection is the fact that when properly interpreted it inspires us to be on a pilgrimage or a perpetual quest. As Christians we are "forever becoming." One who has had a vision of what he should and can become in Christ will be constantly thrilled with the conviction that "the best is yet to be." Most of the creative work in the world is done by restless men and women who have perfection as their goal: "An artist is an artist because he attempts more than he can do."[11] Likewise, God's creative men and women are those who are stirred from within by a dream that causes them to attempt more than they can do or be. They are never satisfied, but they are not frustrated and defeated. They believe that the One who gives the dream is understanding of the dreamer and forgives him for his failures.

As John Calvin said: "Our labour is not lost when today is better than yesterday."[12] Can we say with Paul, "Forgetting what lies behind and straining forward to what lies ahead, I press on toward the goal" (Phil. 3:13–14)? These words picture the runner as he strains forward seeking to win the race. One translation says, "So I run straight toward the goal" (TEV). In this Christian race there is not just one winner. There is just one prize but that one prize is shared by all who run.

FOR THOUGHT AND DISCUSSION

1. In response to the question, "What is Christian perfection?" John Wesley answered: "Loving God with all your heart, mind, soul, and strength. This implies. . .that all the thoughts, words, and actions are governed by pure love." To the question, "Does this exclude the possibility of a mistake?" his answer was, "No." He further said that "a mistake in judgment may possibly occasion a mistake in practice. . .yet, where every word and action springs from love, such mistake is not properly a sin" (*A Plain Account of Christian Perfection*, pp. 42–43). Analyze and appraise.

2. In addition to the scriptures used in the chapter, it might be helpful for you to consider the fruit of the Spirit in Galatians 5:22–23. Ask yourself how much of the fruit of the Spirit you have in your life. If you graded your perfection or maturity on the basis of the fruit of the Spirit, what grades would you make? Would it be an A, B, C, D, or F? Would you grade considerably higher on some fruit than on others?

3. While it is not related to the idea of perfection, what is your judgment concerning the shortened work week which seems inevitable? Some business and industrial concerns have already shortened to four days a week. In the near future, so it is claimed, a man in one seven-hour day will be able to produce as much as he can now produce in a full work week. What effect will the shortened work week have on workers? on our churches? on our society? May the churches have to make some adjustments in their programs? It has been said that what the American worker does with his lei-

sure time will determine the destiny of our nation. What is your judgment?

X

Its Crowning Virtue: Love

There are three Greek words translated "love." They are *eros*, which is not found in the New Testament, *philia*, found approximately twenty-five times in noun and verb forms, and *agape* and *agapao*, found approximately thirty times in the synoptic gospels and twenty-four times in the general epistles, with ten of those in 1 Peter. In contrast, *agape* and *agapao* are found 112 times in the Pauline epistles and 113 times in the Johannine writings. *Agape* is the distinctly New Testament word for love.

Love: Its Meaning

Eros is a seeking, searching love. To use a term of C. S. Lewis, it is a need-love. It is used to describe sexual love but not exclusively so. Barth suggests that "in its purest form it is an impulse from below upwards, from man to what is above him, to the divine." But "in any case. . .it is not a turning to the other for the other's sake, but the satisfying of the vital hunger of the one who loves, for whom the beloved, whether a thing, a man, or the divine, is only as it were consumer goods, the means to an end."[1] The distinctive element in *eros* is that it reaches out to find the fulfillment of some need. It is a grasping, possessive love. *Philia* refers primarily to a warm type of love such as a friend for a friend. It is a shared love.

Agape is unmotivated by anything outside of itself.[2] It is unconditional; it has no reservations. It is uncoerced. It gives itself voluntarily and unselfishly to the object loved.

It is a gift-love. It speaks the language of self-denial and self-sacrifice: "God so loved the world that he *gave* his only Son. . ." (John 3:16); "Christ loved the church and *gave* himself up for her" (Eph. 5:25); "Greater love has no man than this, that a man *lay down* his life for his friends" (John 15:13). There is inherent in *agape* love, to use a Barthian expression, "radically unlimited liberality." Or, as Brunner says, "It is not a love that judges worth, but a love which bestows worth."[3] It will even suffer itself to become "a lost love," a love that may not be returned but which may be rejected and trampled under foot. It does not depend on the response of the one who is loved. It does not refer primarily to the emotions; it operates basically in the area of the will. Some scholars believe that it would have been better to have brought the word into the English language rather than to have translated it.

The type of love expressed by the word *agape* finds full expression only in God. God is *agape*. It expresses the very essence of his being. His love is a gift-love in contrast to a need-love. The nature of this divine love (*agape*) is most fully revealed or manifested in the cross (see 1 John 4:9–10).

On the other hand, man's love at its best is a mixture of gift-love and need-love. Reinhold Niebuhr, in his typically paradoxical or dialectical way, says that *agape* is an "impossible possibility" for man. The awareness that we fall short creates within us a tension that moves us in the direction of *agape*. The latter is the norm for the Christian life. The remainder of this chapter will be a discussion of *agape*, the distinctly Christian concept of love.

Love and the Virtues

Looked at from within the individual, love is a virtue or a character trait. Looked at from outside the individual, love is a principle that provides guidance for the Christian in times of decision. Whether we consider love a virtue or a principle, it stands out as the greatest or crowning virtue or as the most important and most inclusive principle. Does this mean that love is inclusive of all the other virtues or stands alone as a guiding principle for the Christian? The answer is clearly, No. Love is the ground for the other virtues. It gives unity to them, but it does not absorb or eliminate them. It may be and is the mother of the virtues, but children exist as really as the mother. Love is the first but not the only fruit of the Spirit (Gal. 5:22–23). The fact that it is first suggests that it is the most important fruit of the Spirit and that it infuses and gives unity to the others. It should be remembered, however, that as important as love is, the other virtues or qualities are mentioned. Fletcher goes so far as to say that love "is the one and only *regulative principle* of Christian ethics."[4] It is the most important regulative principle but not the only one.

Love may be "the final criterion of righteousness" but it is not the only criterion. It may be the one commandment that is repeated "with magnificent monotony" but it is not the only commandment. Love "binds everything together in perfect harmony" (Col. 3:14) but in the bundle, it binds together compassion, kindness, lowliness, meekness, patience, forbearance, and forgiveness. It may be and is the more or most excellent way (1 Cor. 12:31) but it is not the only way. Love is greater than faith and hope, but they, along with love, abide (1 Cor. 13:13).

The so-called theological virtues—faith, hope, love—are frequently grouped together in Paul's epistles. To the Colossians he wrote, "We have heard of your faith in Christ Jesus and of the love which you have for all the saints, because of the hope laid up for you in heaven" (Col. 1:4–5). He thanked the Lord for the "work of faith and labor of love and steadfastness of hope" of the Thessalonians (1

Thess. 1:3). Faith enables us to overcome the world (1 John 5:4), love to minister to it, and hope to renounce it.

Faith and love are particularly closely related. "The love the Christian has is really not his but the love of God expressed through him. Our response to God's love for us is our faith in him. Through this faith we have come into a vital relationship with the real source of the love that partakes of the divine quality (*agape*). In turn, through faith we become a channel for his love to others—faith works through love (Gal. 5:6), is 'active in love' (NEB), or 'expresses itself in love' (Phillips)."[5] Barth expresses the relation of faith and love as follows: "As we come to faith we begin to love. If we did not begin to love, we would not have come to faith."[6] Love is grounded in or is the product of faith. Faith finds its fulfillment or realization through love. Faith, strictly speaking, is not a virtue but the source or ground of virtues.

A wonderful ladder or stair-step of Christian virtues or character traits is found in 2 Peter 1:5–7. The opening words of the exhortation are: "For this very reason," which clearly refers to something previously said. The author had suggested that his readers had escaped from the corruption that was in the world and had "become partakers of the divine nature" (v. 4). Because this was true or "for this very reason" they should "make every effort to supplement" their "faith with virtue." Here is the therefore perspective so prevalent in the Scriptures. The beginning point is faith; the crowning virtue or quality is *agape*. The latter even stands above love of the brethren or "brotherly affection" (*philadelphia*). *Agape* may be cultivated within and evolve from the Christian fellowship, but it cannot be limited to that fellowship. Its very nature demands that it reach out to all men.

What about the relation of love to one particular virtue: justice? We can believe in the close relation of the two without equating them as Fletcher does: "Love and justice are the same, for justice is love distributed, nothing else."[7]

Tillich suggests that love is the basic or ultimate principle in justice, while justice is imminent in love. Love "shows justice what to do" while "justice is the form and structure of love. . . . Love makes justice just."[8] The creative element in justice is love. Reinhold Niebuhr suggests that "love is both the fulfillment and the negation of all achievements of justice in history."[9] He contends that love cannot maintain itself in human society, but that justice is an attainable goal. This does not mean that love is not relevant. It stands in constant judgment against the very imperfect expressions of love in society. Love is normative for all of life, including justice. *Agape* love is always more than just. Justice is concerned with what is due, *agape* gives itself unselfishly and fully to the one who is loved. It goes beyond justice, operating in the area of grace. "Love can only do more, it can never do less, than justice requires."[10]

Love is basic and primary. Justice is a derivative of love, but it is also an indispensable instrument or expression of love. Love demands justice; it is also the ground for the judgment of justice. Divorce justice from love and it becomes a "soulless legalism." Divorce love from justice and it becomes less than *agape*; it will become a superficial sentimentality.

Love and the Law

The leaders of situation ethics can be commended for the prominence they give to love. We cannot agree, however, with some of the things they say concerning law and the relation of love to law. Fletcher, for example, claims that love is "the solitary law" which should be "understood as the successor to the commandments and not a compressor." Referring to the last six of the Ten Commandments, he goes so far as to say, "Situation ethics has good reason to hold it as a *duty* in some situations to break them, *any or all of them.*"[11]

Those who would, in the name of love, eliminate law should be reminded that love itself is a law or a command. According to James, it is "the royal law" (James 2:8). Jesus called it "a new commandment" (John 13:34). He also plainly said, "If you love me, you will keep my commandments" (John 14:15; cf. 15:10), and there is more than one commandment.

Love to God and neighbor is an act of obedience although it is an obedience that is motivated by love. Love is commanded, yet it is free. Love is the one supreme commandment but not "the solitary" commandment or law. The other commandments, including the Decalogue, will help one to know what the love of God demands in a particular situation.

When Jesus was asked which was "the great commandment in the law," he quoted Deuteronomy 6:5 and then said, "This is the great and first commandment." Notice that love is "the great and *first* commandment," which clearly suggests that it is not the only commandment. He then quoted Leviticus 19:8: "Love your neighbor as yourself" (see Matt. 22:36–39). There follows the statement: "The whole Law of Moses and the teachings of the prophets depend on these two commandments" (v. 40, TEV).

What is meant when it says that the law and the prophets "depend on" or are hung on these two commandments? We may not know the depth of the meaning but evidently it means that all the commandments in the Old Testament scriptures would be fulfilled if one loved God supremely and his neighbor as himself. For example, if one loved God supremely, he would keep the first table of the Law; if he loved his neighbor as himself he would keep the second table of the Law. And the Ten Commandments summarize the requirements of the basic moral law of the Old Testament. It is Paul who says, "The whole law is fulfilled in one word, 'You shall love your neighbor as yourself' " (Gal. 5:14). To reverse Fletcher's statement, the two commandments of love for God and neighbor compress, but they do not succeed or replace the law of Moses or the teachings of the prophets. Kierkegaard suggests that "there is not one provision of the law, not a single one, which love wishes to abolish."[12] Or, as John A. T. Robinson, who is more balanced than Fletcher concerning the relation of love and law, says, "Love builds on law, it comes to fulfil it, not to destroy it; the second mile of love presupposes the first mile of law."[13]

How does love fulfill the law? It fulfills it not by abrogating it but by going beyond it. Jesus said, "Think not that I have come to abolish the law and the prophets; I have come not to abolish them but to fulfil them" (Matt. 5:17). He fulfilled them or gave them "real meaning" (TEV) by going beyond the surface or formal requirements of the law. We see this pointedly brought out in his comparisons in the Sermon on the Mount.

They had heard it said:	*Jesus said*:
No murder	No anger
No adultery	No adulterous thoughts
Divorce for some	No divorce
No false oaths	No oaths
An eye for an eye	No retaliaton
Love neighbor	Love enemy.

Kierkegaard compares the relation of law and love to a sketch and the finished work of art by the same artist. Law and love are from the same source; they are products of the same Artist, and are not at variance any more than the sketch and the finished work of art. He also suggests that there is no more conflict between law and love than between hunger and that which satisfies the hunger.[14]

Some contend that love frees the Christian from the law; that we are under grace and not under law. Theoretically this is correct, but the only people who can be free from the law are those who live beyond the reach of law. Freedom from the law and from any other external authority is realized only when the law is internalized. Such freedom comes as the love of God enters into and controls our lives. Freedom may be the birthright of the Christian, but it is a birthright that must be achieved. The freedom that the Christian has in the love of God is not a freedom from obligation and responsibility. Rather, it is freedom for obligation and service. The well-known word of Luther was:

> A Christian man is a perfectly free lord of all, subject to none.
> A Christian man is a perfectly dutiful servant of all, subject to all.

One of the weaknesses of the so-called new morality or situation ethics is that it assumes a maturity that is unrealistic. Certainly laws and principles play an important part in the moral training of children. And to a distressing degree all of us are children in our understanding of our moral and spiritual responsibilities. We need all the assistance that is available in any time of decision. We may want to do the "loving thing" in a particular situation, but how can we know what love would dictate? As Paul Tillich says, "Every individual, even the most creative, needs given structures that embody the experience and wisdom of the past, that liberate him from the necessity of having to make innumerable decisions on his own, and that show him a meaningful way to act in most situations."[15]

Love: Its Source

What is the source of Christian love, the kind of love that can only be described by the frequently used New Testament word *agape*? The source of such love is not men but God, who is *agape*. Paul wrote to the Romans as follows: "God's love has been poured into our hearts through the Holy Spirit which has been given to us" (Rom. 5:5; cf. Col. 1:8). Again he plainly says that the fruit of the Spirit is love (Gal. 5:22); love "is the gracious gift of the Holy Spirit" (Barth). It is the greatest gift of the Spirit because it is the sharing of the very nature of God. If the Spirit dwells within us there inevitably will be some fruit of the Spirit, including love. We must admit, however, that the fruit may be only thirty or sixty-fold, but there will be and must be some fruit.

One reason we say this is because of the nature of the Christian experience. When we became children of God, we were brought into union with the resurrected Christ. Christ himself said that he and the Father were one. The one with whom we were brought into union through our faith in Christ is love or *agape* (1 John 4:8, 16). Just as surely as the resurrected Christ lives within us, love or *agape* dwells within us. It is this love that constrains or controls us (2 Cor. 5:14). This love "has its origin not in us but in God" (Bonhoeffer). Or, as Kagawa once said, "Our love is the mainspring that God has wound up." This love which is God's creation not only finds lodgment within us but it seeks to reach out through us and touch and bless the lives of others. "We love, because he first loved us" (1 John 4:19); divine love precedes human love. The latter is always the product of and the response to the former.

The fact that our love, as Christians, is expressive of our gratitude to God for his love to us means that the motive for what we do for our fellowmen flows from within. As Kierkegaard says, "As the peaceful lake is grounded deep in the hidden spring which no eye can see, so a man's love is grounded even deeper in the love of God." Similarly, Luther says that Christian love is "a flowing love, which flows from the inside of the heart like a fresh stream that goes on flowing and cannot be stopped or dried up." That flowing stream of love expresses itself in every relation of life: in the home and church, on the campuses and the athletic field, on the streets and in the community, everywhere. In so far as love does not find a normal and natural expression in and through our lives, to that degree we have not let the love of God possess us.

The clearer our awareness of the grace of God expressed through his love for us, the deeper will be our desire to express his love in relation to those about us. In other words, the deeper our sense of forgiveness, the greater will be our love not only for him but also for those he loves. From the background of the woman of the street who had bathed the feet of Jesus with her tears and wiped them with her hair, in marked contrast to the neglect of Simon, Jesus said, "He who is forgiven little, loves little" (Luke 7:47). So it is with us. If we are conscious of having been forgiven much by the Lord, we will not only love him in return but we will also let his love flow through us to bless the lives of others.

And let us suggest again that the more mature we become in him the less we will be conscious of any motive that impels us. What we do for him and for our fellowman will increasingly flow naturally from a deepening and an increasingly vital union with the risen and indwelling Christ. But we must confess that we are all very immature. For this reason, we must continue to make conscious efforts to be and to do what we should. Love (*agape*) has not yet fully possessed our lives. This is one reason why there is still an important place in the Christian life for the imperative as well as the indicative, for the "thou shall nots" as well as the "thou shalls."

Love: Its Dimensions

Paul wrote to the Ephesians as follows: "I pray that you. . .may have the power to understand how broad and long and high and deep is Christ's love. Yes, may you come to know his love—although it can never be fully known" (Eph. 3:17–19, TEV). This sets forth the dimensions of the love of Christ which can never be fully known or expressed in our lives.

Jesus summed up the dimensions of our love in terms of love for God and love for neighbor. These represent the vertical and horizontal phases of life. Concerning the horizontal dimension of love, Barth says, "It will not take place without love of God. And there would be no love to God if it did not take place. But while it can only follow, and must follow, this prior love, it is an autonomous loving, for God in heaven and the neighbour on earth are two and not one." He further says, "Love to others cannot exhaust itself in love to God, nor can love to God exhaust itself in love to others. The one cannot be replaced and made unnecessary by the other."[16]

We have a unique responsibility to love those within the Christian community or fellowhsip. The members of a family should love all people but have a unique love for those within the family circle; so it is or should be in the Christian family. The "new commandment" that Jesus gave his disciples was that they love one another as he had loved them. Most of what Paul and John had to say concerning love was love expressed within the Christian fellowship. This was inevitable since they wrote primarily to Christians and Paul in particular wrote to Christian churches or groups. Paul prayed that the Thessalonians might increase "in love to one another and to all men" (1 Thess. 3:12). The love of the

Christian is to move in a constantly expanding circle: the Christian brotherhood, the neighbor, the enemy.

If we love God, we will love our neighbor, and there are no limits to love of neighbor. If we cannot love our neighbor as he is, then we are loving an idea or ideal, and in the final analysis this means that we are loving ourselves. Luther suggests that Christian love says, "I love you, not because you are good or bad; for I draw my love, not from your goodness, as from another's fountain, but from my own little spring, from the Word, which is grafted in my heart and which bids me love my neighbor." He further says that this love "flows out abundantly and is there for all who need it, touching both the good and the bad, friend and foe."[17]

Let us suggest again that our union with the resurrected Christ is the spring or fountain within that flows out to all kinds of people. Jesus, when he walked among men, was the friend of publicans and sinners. He reached out in love to all types of people: men and women, the blind, the sick, the crippled, the demented, as well as the well and healthy. His eyes were always turned to and his heart reached out to people in need. The same thing will be true of us to the degree that we have been captured by his spirit.

One of the most difficult things for most Christians is to love their enemies and yet Jesus plainly said to his disciples, "Love your enemies and pray for those who persecute you" (Matt. 5:44). By this they would show their kinship to their Father who "makes his sun rise on the evil and on the good, and sends rain on the just and on the unjust" (v. 45). "God shows his love for us in that while we were yet sinners Christ died for us" (Rom. 5:8).

Only Christian love or *agape* can reach out and encircle the enemy. There is no limit for *agape* in depth or range. It is a lost love, and its lostness is not seen anywhere more clearly than in the Cross. It is such a lost love, spontaneous and unmotivated by anything outside of itself, that can love all men, including one's enemies. *Agape* seeks to unite the separated, regardless of the basis of the separation: color, culture, moral standards, etc. We should, however, add that this *agape* type of love never finds complete expression in our lives.

There is at least one additional dimension of love that has not been mentioned: self-love. The second commandment, like unto the first, was: "You shall love your neighbor as yourself." Are we commanded to love ourselves? Is there a place for self-love in the Christian's life? In seeking an answer it is wise to remember that Jesus was quoting from the Old Testament. Also, no writer of the New Testament interpreted Jesus as commanding the love of self. It seems that self-love was assumed and was used for comparative purposes. As Calvin says, "Men are naturally prone to excessive self-love. . .there was no need of a law to inflame a love already existing in excess. . . . The Lord has made self-love as it were the standard."[18] We are to love our neighbor as we actually love ourselves. It does not say "more than we love ourselves." Also, this comparison is not attached to the love for God. We should love God better than we love ourselves. If we love God supremely, we will have a respect for self that will be deepened by our awareness of our relation to him. This awareness of his presence will not only deepen our respect for ourselves but it will also deepen our respect for our neighbor. Our neighbor stands in the presence of God with us. We are equal in his sight. We are to love him as we love ourselves. Such a conception of self-love would make it compatible with self-denial and self-sacrifice which is so prominent in the teachings of the New Testament.

Conclusions Concerning Love

The crowning virtue and the guiding principle in every area of human relations should be love. a love that partakes of the divine quality. It should be a love for one another, for our neighbor, even our neighbor who may be our enemy. This love stems from God's love for us and for our neighbor. It should be a love that reaches up to the level of *agape* and finds its highest expression in the Cross. That kind of love expresses itself through redemptive self-sacrifice. It is this *agape*, self-giving type or quality of love that is described as follows in 1 Corinthians 13:

> Love is patient and kind; love is not jealous or boastful; it is not arrogant or rude. Love does not insist on its own way; it is not irritable or resentful; it does not rejoice at wrong, but rejoices in the right. Love bears all things, believes all things, hopes al things, endures all things.
> Love never ends;. . .(1 Cor. 13:4–8a).

We do not possess these qualities fully but are we, in association with the resurrected Christ, making progress? Are they finding expression in our lives more fully from day to day? If they are, then our relations with others in the church, in the home, in the community, and in the world will be constantly improving.

FOR THOUGHT AND DISCUSSION

1. Does it seem to you that some non-Christians manifest the *agape* type of love more than many Christians? Has this ever bothered you? How can it be explained?
2. After an address on "Love and Human Relations" a keen young Negro Ph.D. asked the probing question:

"Is there not a real danger that so-called Christian love will become a mere sentimentality and a substitute for justice?" How would you have answered that question? Would some of the statements made concerning the relation of the two by Brunner, Niebuhr, and Tillich help? Will the *agape* type of love ever do less than justice? Is there, however, a real danger that some will substitute what they call love for justice? Is this true not only in human relations including race relations but also in other relations?

3. What do you think of an unmarried couple who justify their participation in sex relations by saying, "We love one another"? Do you think love that partakes of the *agape* quality would lead to pre-marital sex relations, or would it postpone such relations until after marriage? How would you defend your position?

PART III
CONCLUSIONS CONCERNING THE CHRISTIAN LIFE

Our discussion in Part III will be restricted to two conclusions concerning the Christian life and its ethic. The first of these conclusions (Chap. XI) is that the cross is the unifying symbol of a distinctly Christian life and the more distinctly Christian the more prominent will be the cross. The other conclusion (Chap. XII) is that tension is a continuing, persistent problem for any serious Christian.

These two conclusions are closely related. They, to a considerable degree, are integral parts of one another. For example, tension that contributes to the redemptive purpose of God in the world can properly be considered a phase of one's taking up a cross and following Christ. On the other hand, one who voluntarily and consistently takes up his cross or crucifies himself will discover that the cross creates tension within him and also between him and the world in which he lives. Sometimes this tension will be felt even within his family and within the church, his spiritual family.

We can sum up by simply saying that the more serious one is about being a real rather than a nominal Christian, the more the cross and tension will become realities in his life.

XI

Its Unifying Symbol: The Cross

When we say that the cross is the unifying symbol of the Christian life we do not mean to imply that it is merely a symbol. It is a symbol but it is much more. It is also a historic event. That was a very real cross on which Christ died. The reality of that cross gives depth and meaning to the cross as a symbol of the kind of life we should live for Christ in the world.

Christ and His Cross

What do we think about or visualize when we hear or see the words "the cross"? Most of us doubtlessly see or visualize a cross on a hill outside Jerusalem, or we may see three crosses with the central one a little more prominent than the others. Most of us tend to relate the cross almost exclusively to the death of Christ. We do not mean by the preceding to deprecate one iota the death of Christ on the cross. His death, along with his resurrection, is the central event of both human and divine history.

Jesus, however, not only died on the cross, he also lived the cross-like life and in that way as well as by his death he revealed God and was a redemptive influence among men. He went about doing good, giving himself unselfishly in service to those about him. "The whole historical life of Jesus was the way of the Cross" (Brunner).

One incident in the life of Jesus clearly reveals that he paid a price for his ministry to the needs of people. He was on his way to the house of Jairus whose daughter was dying.

People were pressing and crowding him on every side. In the crowd was a woman who had had a "flow of blood" or a "severe bleeding" (TEV) for twelve years (Luke 8:43). No one had been able to help her. She slipped up behind Jesus and touched the fringe, edge, or hem of his garment and was immediately healed. Jesus, looking around, said, "Who was it that touched me?" When no one acknowledged that he had touched him, Peter said to him, "Master, the multitudes surround you and press upon you." In other words, many people were touching him. How did Jesus know that the woman had touched him? He revealed the reason he knew when he replied to Peter: "Some one touched me; for I perceive that power has gone forth from me" (Luke 8:46). There was one in the pressing crowd who received a blessing from him. This could not be true without power flowing from him to her.

His death on the cross was in a very real sense a continuation of the type and quality of life he had lived. His incarnation really involved the cross. For example, Paul says: "For our sake he made him [Christ] to be sin who knew no sin, so that in him we might become the righteousness of God" (2 Cor. 5:21). Again Paul says: "For you know the grace of our Lord Jesus Christ, that though he was rich, yet for your sake he became poor, so that by his poverty you might become rich" (2 Cor. 8:9).

We can properly speak of the atoning life of Christ as well as of his atoning death. He is the atoning person. At least his death cannot be separated from his life. The former was the more or less natural culmination of the life he had lived. Symbolic of the life he had lived, he was crucified between two thieves. While among men he associated with and ministered to the publicans and sinners.

The cross or something closely akin to it or symbolized by it was central in a number of the decisive or crisis experiences in the life of Jesus. Such experiences frequently reveal the motivating influences in one's life and/or his dominant values.

The baptism of Jesus was a decisive experience (Matt. 3:13–17). Through his baptism he identified himself with sinful men. At that time the heavens were opened and the Spirit descended like a dove and lit upon him and a voice from heaven said, "This is my beloved Son, with whom I am well pleased" (cf. Matt. 17:5). This statement of the voice from heaven may have caused the mind of Jesus to recall the familiar words of one of the messianic psalms:

> I will tell of the decree of the Lord:
> He said to me, "You are my son, today I have begotten
> you"
>
> (Ps. 2:7).

The entire incident, and particularly the descending of the Spirit as the dove, likely also reminded Jesus of the following verse in Isaiah, a favorite book of his:

> Behold my servant, whom I uphold, my chosen, in whom
> my soul delights;
> I have put my spirit upon him,
> He will bring forth justice to the nations
>
> (Isa. 42:1).

If Jesus thought of this statement, he doubtlessly identified himself with the suffering servant so prominent in the later chapters of Isaiah.

Immediately following the baptism came the temptation, another crisis or decisive experience in the life of Jesus. One, if not the main, point of the temptation story was that Jesus accepted the Father's way for his messiahship which meant suffering and the cross. He chose the road that went by way of Calvary followed by the empty tomb.

Another experience of Jesus which has been referred to as the "watershed of the Gospel" was his conversation with his disciples at Caesarea Philippi. It was there that he began to reveal to them more clearly than he had previously that he had to go to Jerusalem and there suffer many things from the chief priests, the scribes, and the elders (the three groups in the Sanhedrin), and be put to death and on the third day rise again. It was from this background that Jesus said, "If any man would come after me, let him deny himself and take up his cross and follow me" (Matt. 16:24).

A week after Caesarea Philippi there is recorded the experience on the Mount of Transfiguration when Moses representing the Law and Elijah representing the Prophets talked with Jesus about his coming departure "which he was to accomplish at Jerusalem" (Luke 9:31).

There is no record of what transpired between Caesarea Philippi and the Mount of Transfiguration. It is a "silent week." What do you suppose happened during the week? Since the main topic of conversation at Caesarea Philippi and on the Mount of Transfiguration was the cross or his death, it seems logical to believe that during the week he continued to try to help the disciples to understand that he had to go to Jerusalem and die on a cross. He doubtlessly also attempted to make it increasingly clear to them that they had to take up their crosses if they were to follow him.

Still another crisis or decisive experience in the life of Jesus took place in the Garden of Gethsemane (Matt. 26:36–46). The cross was clearly the central reality in this experience. It, with all of its meaning, was immediately ahead. He took with him the same three disciples who had shared with him the transfiguration experience and went apart from the others. He said to the three, "My soul is very sorrowful, even to death; remain here, and watch with me" (v. 38). He then went "a little farther" into the Garden of Suffering; the last few steps had to be taken alone. From the beginning of his prayer, there was submission to the Father. He said, "My Father, if it be possible, let this cup pass from me" (v. 39: the "cup" was a symbol of great suffering). It was not death that made him cry out but the crushing weight of the sin of the sons of men upon his own sinless heart. There follows the "nevertheless, not as I will, but as thou wilt," which is the epitome of real prayer. Here the cross of Calvary was accepted. Following Gethsemane there was the actual crucifixion followed by the glorious resurrection. But without the victory in Gethsemane there would have been no Golgotha and no empty tomb.

The Christian and His Cross

It is proper that we should include the cross in our songs. It is unfortunate, however, that we sing of an "old rugged cross *on a hill far away*." The latter expression reveals rather accurately the entirely too prevalent attitude toward the cross. Most of us want no part of it. We are obsessed with the idea that the cross is for Christ, a once-and-for-all thing in the past tense. Although there is a sense in which the cross of Christ is "once for all" (see Heb. 9:12, 28; 10:10), it "is continually trying to make itself visible in contemporary situations." [1] It is made visible, at least to a limited degree, through the lives of those who have come to the Christ of the cross and who, in turn, have taken up their cross and are following him. The "limited degree" in the preceding sentence stems from the fact that their cross is not his cross. "It is a matter of similarity in great dissimilarity." [2] Or, again as Barth says, "What they suffer is not what Jesus suffered. . . . They exist only. . .in the echo of His sentence, the shadow of His judgment, the after-pains of His rejection." [3]

The cross, when properly understood, is not exclusively for Christ nor exclusively a thing of the past tense. Jesus is not supposed to "bear the cross alone and all the world go free. No, there's a cross for everyone, and there's a cross for [you and] me." Bonhoeffer's frequently quoted statement is: "When Christ calls a man, He bids him come and die." [4] What Jesus had attempted to teach his disciples came vividly alive with a new and deeper meaning for them after his crucifixion and resurrection.

What do we mean when we say that the Christian must take up his cross to follow Christ? It does not mean the wearing of a cross around the neck or in the lapel of a coat. Neither does it refer to suffering or some burden that comes through the operation of the laws of nature. How often we hear people say when some great sorrow or some great personal suffering comes upon them, "I guess this is my cross; I will have to bear it." This is not the basic meaning of the cross for the Christian, although the victorious acceptance of and adjustment to such suffering may be used by the Lord to bless the lives of many people.

A cross is something on which one is crucified. Crucifixion means suffering, but all suffering cannot be identified with the taking up of a cross, with Christian crucifixion. Suffering which can be identified with the cross must be, among other things, suffering that is accepted for the sake of Christ and his cause. Its purpose and ultimate end must be redemptive, although in the deepest sense only the suffering of Christ on the cross is redemptive.

What does it mean in a more specific way for one to take up a cross? As suggested earlier, a cross is something on which one dies. It involves for the Christian the crucifixion of self with selfish ambitions and purposes. As Brunner says, "To be 'in Christ' means the death of the selfish Ego. It means the moritification of that will whose poison penetrates the whole of our nature," [5] or it means "giving oneself up to Christ and his will as Christ gave himself up to God and his will." [6] It may mean walking an unknown path, but how grateful we should be that we walk with a known Companion who has walked that path before us! As we walk with the Christ of the cross, we have a deepening insight into the meaning and nature of the cross and find ourselves increasingly living in the spirit of the cross.

Paul, who had an important place for "the cross of Christ" in his epistles gives considerable insight into the meaning of the cross or crucifixion for the Christian.[7] He says that "those who belong to Christ have crucified the flesh ["lower nature," NEB] with its passions and desires" (Gal. 5:24). He also says that the world had been crucified to him and he to the world (Gal. 6:14). Still again he says that "our old self ["the man we once were," NEB] was crucified with him" (Rom. 6:6; for additional references see 2 Cor. 1:5; 4:10; Phil. 3:8, 10; Col. 1:24). The nearest thing to a definition in the Bible of crucifixion or cross-bearing for a Christian is the following statement by Paul: "I have been crucified with Christ; it is no longer I who live, but Christ who lives in me" (Gal. 2:20). Paul could go so far as to say "for me to live is Christ" (Phil. 1:21). We cannot say that, but it should be the desire of our hearts that we move in that direction.

While Jesus did not set forth specifically the meaning of the Christian's cross, except that it involved self-denial, he did spell out in general terms its nature. By comparing the accounts in Matthew (16), Mark (8), and Luke (9) of the conversation at Caesarea Philippi we discover the following concerning the Christian and his cross: (1) Taking up the cross is voluntary: "*if any man would* come after me." The cross is not laid on the shoulder of the disciple; it is taken up. (2) It is necessary: "if any man would *come after* me." We do not have to take up the cross; he will not force it on us, but we must take up our cross if we are to follow him. This emphasis is not only found at Caesarea Philippi but also in other conversations he had with his disciples (see Matt. 10:38; Luke 14:27). There is no real discipleship without the cross, or, as Bonhoeffer says, "Just as Christ is

Christ only in virtue of His suffering and rejection, so the disciple is a disciple only in so far as he shares His Lord's suffering and rejection and crucifixion. . . . In other words it means the cross." [8] (3) Taking up a cross is personal: "if *any* man." (4) It is also universal. Here the three synoptic gospels combined give us a very graphic picture. Mark 8:34 says that "he called to him the multitude with his disciples, and said to them. . ." Luke 9:23 says, "and he said to all." Taking up the cross does not apply exclusively to the missionary, to the pastor, or to others in church-related vocations. It applies to all of God's children. (5) One other great truth concerning the taking up of the cross is revealed by an examination of Luke's account of Caesarea Philippi. According to Luke, Jesus said, "If any man would come after me, let him deny himself and take up his cross daily and follow me" (Luke 9:23). It is a daily or continuing experience.

Results of Taking up the Cross

We have discussed quite briefly the meaning of the cross for the Christian and the nature of his cross-bearing. There is one other aspect of the Christian and his cross that we should consider. It is tremendously significant from the viewpoint of everyday Christian living. Let us formulate it as a question: what are the results of a Christian taking up his cross? We will discover the answer to this question by reviewing briefly the relation of the cross and the purposes of God in the life of Christ. As suggested earlier, Christ came to reveal God to man, to reveal his love for man and also his hatred of sin. Man could never have known fully either of these had Christ not died on the cross. It is John who says, "By this we know love, that he laid down his life for us" (1 John 3:16). The cross also elicits or produces a love that must be shared with others. One reason for this is the fact that the love expressed in the cross is not exclusively for us but for all men. Men around us will come to know that kind of love to the degree that we, in response to his love for us, take up our cross and follow him.

Also, as we take up a cross and follow him we will find life for ourselves. Immediately after his invitation at Caesarea Philippi for the disciples to deny self and take up the cross and follow him, he said, "For whoever would save his life will lose it, and whoever loses his life for my sake will find it" (Matt. 16:25; cf. 10:39, John 12:25). Similarly, Paul says, "If we have died with Christ, we believe that we shall also live with him" (Rom. 6:8). The cross is not only a symbol of death but also of life.

Another way of stating this same great truth is to say that resurrection follows crucifixion. Oscar Cullman says we should write it crucifixion-resurrection. Jesus told the disciples that he had to go to Jerusalem and suffer many things and be killed and "on the third day be raised" (Matt. 16:21). His resurrection was mentioned in the same breath as his crucifixion. So it is with the child of God. Bonhoeffer's frequently quoted statement is that "Jesus Christ and His call are necessarily our death and our life."[9] Death comes first, then life, but there is no real crucifixion without resurrection. Here is one of the marvelous paradoxes of the Gospel: life comes through death, but it has to be a real death or crucifixion, without any motivation beyond the crucifixion itself. There is no place here for self-seeking self-denial, for crucifixion with the expectation of resurrection.

There is one other glorious result of the Christian's cross-bearing. He will not only find life in its fullness, he also will be a source of life to others. Jesus came to redeem man as well as to reveal God. We cannot redeem men but we can be a redeeming influence among men. This we will be as we deny self, take up our cross, and follow him. In John 12 immediately preceding the statement by Jesus that "he who loves his life loses it," he said, "Unless a grain of wheat falls into the earth and dies, it remains alone ["a single grain," Ph.]; but if it dies, it bears much fruit" ("a rich harvest," NEB) (v. 24). Later in the same conversation he said, "And I, when I am lifted up from the earth, will draw all men to myself" (v. 32). In verse 24 is found the basic law of God's universe: new life comes through death. In verse 25 it is applied to human relations, while in verse 32 it is applied to the spiritual order. We give life to others as we give our own lives in unselfish devotion to them and to our heavenly Father.

Since none of us is perfect we are forced to say that to the degree that we deny self, to the degree that we take up our cross, to that degree and that degree only we will reveal God and his power, will discover life abundant, and will be a source of life and blessing to others.

The Cross and Other Aspects of the Christian Life

In Part II it was suggested that the Christian life is so broad and varied that no one term can adequately describe its ethic. It is clear, however, that the cross is the one symbol or general principle that most nearly unifies, ties into one bundle, and illuminates the various aspects or approaches to the Christian life and its ethic.

For example, if the dominant motive of the Christian's life is the glory of God (Chap. VI), it will mean the denial of self, expressed in the taking up of a cross. Similarly, one will move toward perfection or full maturity (Chap. IX) as he walks in fellowship with the crucified and risen Christ. We will walk with him only as and to the degree that we deny self and take up our cross and follow him. Other terms are used to describe the Christian ethic such as an ethic of the Holy Spirit, a *koinonia* ethic, a covenant ethic, and a commitment ethic. Each of these would require the denial of self and the taking up of a cross.

Let us spell out a little more fully the relation of the cross to the will of God as the source of authority (Chap. VII), to the kingdom of God as the supreme value (Chap. VIII), and to love as the crowning virtue (Chap. X) of the Christian life.

There was evidently a close relation between the will of God and the cross in the life of Christ. You remember the incident at Jacob's well (John 4:1–42). Jesus was weary and stayed at the well while his disciples went into town for food. He had had the conversation with the Samaritan woman during which he had introduced her to the living water. When the disciples returned and offered him food, he declined and said to them, "I have food to eat of which you do not know" (v. 32). They thought possibly someone had brought him food. His word to them was, "My food is to do ["obey," TEV] the will of him who sent me, and to accomplish his work" (v. 34). On another occasion he said, "I seek not my own will but the will of him who sent me" (John 5:30; cf. John 6:38). Here is the language of self-giving, of self-denial or cross-bearing. The cross for Jesus represented the last step of submission to the Father's will.

What is true in the life of the Master should be true in the life of his follower: we should not seek our own will but the will of him who has sent us. What Jesus said after his resurrection to the small group of disciples he would say to all of us, "As the Father has sent me, even so I send you" (John 20:21). He was sent; we are sent. He was sent to do the Father's will; we are sent to do his will. He was sent to reveal God; we are sent to reveal him. He was God incarnate; we are to be Christ incarnate. He was sent to redeem man; we are sent to be a redeeming influence among men.

To accomplish all that he was sent to do meant the cross. To accomplish all that he has sent us to do, likewise means the cross for us.

Another of the central concepts in the life and teachings of Jesus was the kingdom of God. Some consider it the key idea or watchword of his earthly ministry and of his movement in general. The disciple of Christ is to seek first the kingdom of God and his righteousness (Matt. 6:33). The reign, the rule, or the kingdom of God is to be sought before wealth and material things, even before the necessities of life. Jesus promised that the latter would be added if his followers put the kingdom first.

In the wonderful parables about the kingdom there are two that are particularly pertinent for our purpose. Jesus said the kingdom was like a treasure hid in a field or it was like a merchant in search of fine pearls. The disciple is to sell or give up all that he has for the sake of the kingdom. Here is involved self-denial or the taking up of a cross.

The close relation of love *(agape)* and the cross is equally clear. As suggested previously, *agape* is self-giving, it speaks the language of the cross. The cross is the supreme demonstration, manifestation, or proof of the love of God. It is at the cross that we most fully know that God is love. In turn, the child of God is to love God supremely. In what has been termed the exaggerated language of contrast, Jesus on one occasion said, "If anyone comes to me and does not hate his own father and mother and wife and children and brothers and sisters, yes, even his own life, he cannot be my disciple" (Luke 14:26). The words immediately following the preceding are: "Whoever does not bear his own cross and come after me, cannot be my disciple." Evidently supreme love for Christ and the bearing of a cross are equated.

Furthermore, Christians are to love one another. How much? Jesus said, "As I have loved you" (John 15:12). How much had he loved them and how much does he love us: enough to give his life on the cross. We are to lay down our lives for the brethren (1 John 3:16).

We are not only to love our fellow Christians, we are to love our neighbor, and he is anyone in need. This love is even to reach out to enemies. Surely such love necessitates self-denial, self-sacrifice symbolized by the cross. It is the *agape* type or quality of love that has this spirit of self-giving.

The cross, "the supreme paradox of all time," as a symbol expresses and breathes life into some of the great paradoxes of the Gospel. Those paradoxes set forth some of the most significant truths of our Christian faith. They express in different words and ways the fact that resurrection follows crucifixion not only in the life of Christ but also in the life of his disciple. One of those paradoxes stated by Jesus on more than one occasion was that exaltation comes through humility (Matt. 23:1–12; Luke 14:7–11; 18:9–14). He also plainly taught that greatness comes through service (Matt. 20:26–27; 23:11; Mark 9:35) and that life comes through death (Matt. 10:39; 16:25; Mark 8:35; Luke 9:24; 17:33; John 12:25).

Another paradox particularly prevalent in the Pauline epistles is that the free man in Christ is to surrender his freedom and become a slave of Christ and a servant of man. For example, he says, "For you were called to freedom, brethren, only do not use your freedom as an opportunity to the flesh, but through love be servants of one another" (Gal. 5:13). Real freedom comes through enslavement to Christ and his way of life. Without the cross, the preceding and other paradoxes of the gospel would be meaningless.

Application to Life

Just as Christ is our "eternal contemporary," likewise his cross, its message and spirit, is relevant for every age and every problem. It is the cross that reconciles us to one another and "to God in one body." This reconciliation brings "hostility to an end" (Eph. 2:16), whether that hostility is based on national origin, culture, economic class, race, or religion.

The spirit symbolized by the cross is to be applied personally by the Christian. We are not just to talk about it; we are to seek as best we can to take up our cross and follow Christ. This means, among other things, that we are to love our enemies that we may be like our Father who sends rain and sunshine upon the just and the unjust (Matt. 5:43–45). It means that we are not to give primary consideration to what we think is right for us to do, but we are to think in terms of what others think and the effect that our behavior will have upon others and particularly upon the cause of Christ (1 Cor. 10:24, 31). The way of the cross will remain for the best of us an aspiration rather than an actual achievement. But we should seek as best we can to move constantly in it and toward it.

The spirit symbolized by the cross is also to be applied to the broader social relations and problems of life. The cross is central in the Christian social strategy. It is the Christian method of social change. This involves the returning of good for evil, the strong serving the weak, the privileged taking the initiative in working out the problems of the underprivileged, even the just to a degree taking upon themselves the sins of the unjust.

This means that voluntary self-giving with a redemptive purpose or goal which can properly be called an ethic of the cross is abidingly relevant for our world and its problems.

The cross is God's strategy for overcoming sin, not only in the individual's life but also in the life of the world.

Let us briefly apply this to one particular area—the area of race relations. Does it mean that those who belong to the oppressed minority are to bear patiently any injustice and discrimination? Is this their cross? This could be a cross in the Christian sense only if it was accepted voluntarily and if it was redemptive in outcome.

The cross applies in a particular way to the majority, to the powerful, to the privileged. They are the ones who can voluntarily correct the evils or ills of our society. They are the ones to whom the voluntary principle will apply in a special way. The cross for them can mean giving of self, the sacrifice of privilege for the sake, not only of others, but also for the sake of society, and what is more important, for the sake of the cause of Christ.

Changes in society are brought about, in the main, by one of two ways: by pressure and the use of force or by peaceful methods. The latter is the Christian method for change. The only hope for a peaceful solution with a minimum even of social pressure for the contemporary racial crisis, along with other world problems, is that the powerful and privileged will accept the responsibility to find a solution in harmony with the Christian spirit and Christian teachings.

Let us sum up by saying that the cross and what it symbolizes is the central distinctive unifying element in original Christianity, including its ethic. We must in the contemporary period return to this central emphasis, must understand more clearly what the cross means in the Christian's life, and must apply more consistently the ethic of the cross if we are to revitalize contemporary Christianity and make the Christian religion a vital factor in meeting the world's needs. "The way of the cross leads home" for the individual, but it is also the way of social reconstruction and moral reformation.

Furthermore, the cross is the symbol of the fundamental law of God's universe. If we had eyes to see, we would see a cross written at the center of that universe. The first or basic law of life is not self-preservation; it is self-denial and self-sacrifice, it is "the way of the cross." This law is operative in the physical universe and in the social order as well as in the spiritual realm.

FOR THOUGHT AND DISCUSSION

1. Glance back over or think through the preceding chapters. Are there some problems or issues that were mentioned that you did not have time to think through at that time? Are there any on which you have changed your position? If you have changed, in what way and why?

2. What effect will the "ethic of the cross" have on an individual who takes it seriously? Will he become "an easy touch," a mild-mannered individual who can be "run over by others"? Will its effect on him be primarily negative or positive? Will he consider primarily his own rights or the rights of others? What will be the relative importance he gives to his own rights and his responsibility?

3. How do you think the application of the ethic of the cross might apply to a white church in an increasingly black community? What about a black church in a similar situation? What about "white" churches in general? Should they admit blacks and others to their worship services and into their membership? What if this would seriously affect the "fellowship" of a church or cause a split? Should a pastor ever risk losing a

church because of his stand on race or on some other major issue? How are your answers related to the preceding chapters, particularly those on the will of God, the kingdom of God, and love?

XII

Its Continuing Problem: Tension

There are some tensions that a Christian should not have, such as those that result from self-centeredness, immaturity, instability, and/or a lack of faith in the Lord. These tensions are destructive and self-defeating. In extreme form, they may become neurotic compulsions, culminating in nervous and mental disorders.

In this chapter we shall concentrate on constructive rather than destructive tensions. Constructive tensions result from an honest attempt to live a consistent Christian life and to contribute what one can to lifting the world toward God's purposes for it. As a teacher for many years of young preachers, I frequently said to them: "If you want to be nice and warm and comfortable in the ministry, do not get serious about being a real Christian and do not get serious about doing anything about the world in which you live. If you get serious about these things, you will be uncomfortably conscious of falling far short of doing and being what you ought to do and be. You will live under constant tension." This is just as true for the layman as it is for the minister. Tension is natural and inevitable for the serious Christian.

A Backward Look

The fact that constructive tensions stem from the very nature of the Christian life can be seen by a glance at the preceding chapters of this book. Each subject discussed involves the serious searching Christian in tension of some type and to some degree.

For example, man is on a constant search for truth (Chap. I). That search stems, to a large degree, from the fact that he was created in the image of God, that the image was marred by sin, and that man is constantly seeking its restoration. The image is restored through man's union with Christ, who is the exact image of the Father, but it is not completely or perfectly restored. The restoration is a process as well as an achievement. As a process there will continue an inner tug toward its fuller attainment until the end of the journey when we shall awake in his likeness.

Similarly, tension is the natural result of any serious consideration of the subjects discussed in the other chapters. The God we worship, who is a moral Person, expects his children to be like him (Chap. II). At best we fall far short. Even in our relations to our fellowman (Chap. III) we do not measure up to God's expectations. We frequently treat our fellowman as a thing, an it, an instrument or a means rather than an end, a thou, created in the image of God and one for whom Christ died. There is still considerable class and racial prejudice in most of our lives.

When we examine the Scriptures, (Chap. IV) we realize that their expectations are far beyond our present level of living. This is true of the Old Testament but particularly of the New Testament. When we examine the quality of life lived by Jesus, we are deeply conscious of our need for divine help.

That help came to us in a unique way when we were brought into union with the resurrected Christ (Chap. V). We discover, however, that even after that marvelous experience we fail to let him fully live in us and express himself through us. Life for us continues to be imperfect, plagued with inconsistencies and shortcomings. The only Christians who are not conscious of falling short are those who do not clearly understand what the Christian life means or are not thoroughly committed to living a real Christian life. God's best people are usually the very ones who are most dissatisfied with themselves and their present level of living.

Our union with Christ should mean that the fruit of the Christian life would naturally and inevitably evolve from our relation to him. In other words, ideally the fruit is first inner and then outer. We discover, however, that while the indwelling Christ may be the source of the fruit we bear for him that the fruit falls short in quantity and quality of his and even our expectation. We likewise discover that although the Christian life should be lived in the indicative mood, much of it must be actually lived in the imperative mood. There is a continuing conflict and tension between what we do and what we know we ought to do but particularly between what we are and what we are convinced we ought to be.

An examination of the chapters under "The Nature of the Christian Life" will reveal comparable sources of tension. For example, we should be motivated by a desire to glorify God (Chap. VI) in gratitude for what he has done for us. At best our motives are mixed. There are times when it seems that we seek our own glory more than the glory of God. There are similar conflicts regarding the source of authority in our lives (Chap. VII). There may be times when we sincerely seek to know and do the will of God. There are other times when we listen to the voice of our friends, our gang, our community, as well as our own wishes more than we listen for the voice of God.

The kingdom of God is the supreme value of the Christian life (Chap. VIII). It should be sought first by all of God's children. It is the treasure hidden in a field; it is the pearl of great price. Everything in the Christian's life should be subordinated to the kingdom or rule of God, and if need be, given up for it. Will you not agree that frequently we seek first the temporal and material things of this world?

The ultimate ideal for the Christian is perfection (Chap. IX), a perfection measured by the perfection, completeness, wholeness, or maturity found in God. Who would dare say that he measures up to such a high ideal? The resulting tension for the serious Christian is deepened because he is persuaded that the ideal is beyond his ability to attain and even his capacity to comprehend or fully understand.

Certainly love for God and our fellowman is the crowning virtue of the Christian life (Chap. X). But many of us love ourselves not only more than we love our neighbor but also more than we love God. The more fully we understand the nature of *agape*, the distinctive New Testament word for love, the more deeply conscious we become that *agape* finds only incomplete or partial expression in our lives. Our love for God and our fellowman at best is a mixture of a gift-love *(agape)* and a need-love *(eros)*.

What can we say when we consider the cross as the unifying symbol of the Chrstian life (Chap. XI)? If the cross could be restricted to Christ, we might feel little tension regarding it. But Jesus himself pointedly said, "If any man would come after me, let him deny himself and take up his cross daily and follow me" (Luke 9:23). Again he said, "Whoever does not bear his own cross and come after me cannot be my disciple" (Luke 14:27). The initial and continuing invitation of Jesus was and is, "Come, follow me." If we follow him all the way, it will take us through the Garden to the cross. Surely all of us will agree that our crucifixion of self, with selfish motives, purposes, and ambitions is only partial.

We can sum up by saying that every phase of the Christian life, when understood properly and considered seriously, is a creator of tension for the seeking, searching Christian. We should always remember, however, that such tension contributes to our growth in the Christian life: there is no progress without tension.

Additional Reasons for Tension

There are additional reasons for tension, some of which may merely be different ways of stating some of the causes of tension previously mentioned. It has been suggested that tension is a natural, integral part of the Christian life. It would be correct to say that tension, to some degree, is the lot of all men: non-Christians as well as Christians. There are psychological and environmental tensions as well as the more strictly spiritual. There are occasions when the spiritual factors that contribute to tension are closely related to the psychological and environmental factors. There are, for example, tensions for Christians and non-Christians that stem from the fact that each of us is or at least we feel that we are a multiplicity of persons.

> Within my earthly temple there's a crowd.
> There's one of us that's humble; one that's proud.
> There's one that's broken-hearted for his sins,
> And one who, unrepentant, sits and grins.
> There's one who loves his neighbor as himself,
> And one who cares for naught but fame and self.
> From much corroding care would I be free
> If once I could determine which is me.

We are searching for a unity that will give us a sense of oneness or wholeness and will release within us our maximum creative capacities.

Eichrodt, the great German Old Testament scholar, says that "the whole life of the believer is lived under constant tension: the tension between the Now and the Hereafter, between the part and the perfect whole, between defeat and triumph." [1] The Christian lives in two worlds. He is a citizen of the world but also a citizen of the kingdom of God. He may be a stranger here within a foreign land but he is here. He faces in two directions. He looks to God for guidance and for strength, he looks out toward the world and those that live in the world with a desire to serve them in the name of his God. Changing the figure: one hand reaches up or out toward God, the other reaches down or out toward his fellowman. His desire is to bring the two closer together.

The clearer his vision of God and the other world, the sharper will be the contrast and conflict between the part and the perfect whole. The tug within him is toward the perfect, the complete, the whole but at his best he is deeply conscious of his incompleteness or imperfection. Even if one could attain personal perfection, he would feel very ill at ease in our imperfect society. He would also discover that he was quite limited in what he could do to move society toward wholeness or perfection.

One basic conflict that somewhat summarizes all of the preceding is the tension between the ideal and the real, between what we are and what we are persuaded we ought to be. There is a constant tug to come up higher. Without this tug or tension, our lives tend to level off and to become a more or less monotonous routine. The latter will continue unless and until some catastrophe comes into our lives or until something unusual awakens us. On the other hand, the higher the ideal for ourselves the sharper will be the inner conflict between the ideal self and the real self. Furthermore, the more the Christian moves toward his ideal self, the more marked is his conflict with the world in which he lives. He discovers that he not only has a civil war within his own soul; he is also at war with the world. In turn, the war with the world contributes to the inner civil war. He discovers that he has to come to some kind of terms with the world if he is to live in it. And yet he cannot completely accept the world as it is without denying his Christian faith. He knows that if he is to lift the world toward God's purposes for it, he must start with the world where it is but also he must maintain sufficient tension to lift or move the world in the direction in which it ought to go.

We may not like the word, but the preceding procedure or strategy requires some compromise or accommodation. Once we begin to compromise, how far shall we go? If we go too far in accommodating to the real world we not only will deny our Christian profession, we will also lose our capacity to lift the world. Experience has taught the Christian that many decisions, because of the kind of world in which he lives, are in the gray area and not clear-cut decisions between black and white.

Another way to express somewhat the same concept is to suggest, as stated previously, that many times the Christian seemingly has to choose between the lesser-of-two-evils. In other words, the decision involves some black and some white. Such a decision cannot be equated with the intentional will of God. At best, it may be considered a part of his circumstantial will. Every decision in the gray area, every lesser-of-two-evils decision results in some tension for the sensitive Christian. It is such tension, however, that moves the child of God more and more in the direction of the perfect or intentional will of God.

Let us spell out a little more specifically something that has already been implied. The serious Christian is caught, at times, in a frustrating dilemma. He may want, at least in his own personal life and in the principles he professes to follow, to be fully Christian. He is convinced, however, if he goes too far or too fast in applying those principles to the contemporary social situation that he may lose all opportunity to minister to or serve the world. In other words, the tension may become too great between him and his friends, his neighbors, his community, and even his church. He may become thoroughly frustrated. He wants to go all the way right now in applying the Christian ethic and the

Christian spirit, yet he feels that he must compromise, to some degree, or be crucified. And what is more significant, he is not sure that his crucifixion would serve the kingdom of God better than for him to relax the pressure a little, but to continue to maintain the tension in the right direction.

Tension is not only natural and inevitable for the individual Christian, it is also natural for the Christian community or the church. There is some tension within the church that more or less naturally evolves from the fact that it is a divine-human institution. It is divine in its origin, its mission and message. It is human in its constituency and its environment. It inevitably is influenced by both of its natures. If it ministers effectively to people and to the world in which they live, it must begin where they are. On the other hand, it will not lift them unless it maintains a wholesome tension between where they are and where they ought to be. The church should serve both a priestly and a prophetic function. It should be "a refuge for disturbed souls" but also a disturber of souls. Its effort to keep these two functions or aspects of its life and work in balance is a source of tension for the church itself. Also, the church, as a human institution, is under the judgment of its own message as a divine institution. The church needs to recognize that it is not what it ought to be. It needs to let its divine nature express itself more fully.

Tension also arises within the church because its members differ in their insight into the church's message and mission. Some prophetic, creative souls may take the church's message seriously and seek to apply fully and consistently basic Christian teachings to their lives and to the life of the church and the world. Others within the Christian fellowship consider such efforts of the "prophetic" as the work of impractical idealists.

The more the church itself becomes a prophetic community the greater will be the tension between it and the world.

In other words, "the more vigorously and consistently the church preaches, teaches, and practices the Christian ideal, the more tension it will create in the world and among men. A lack of tension between the church and the world would be an indication of an unhealthy condition." [2]

Release of Tension[3]

Notice that we do not say "Cure for Tension." There can be and are sources for the release or relaxing of the kind of tension we are discussing, but there is no complete cure. Does the Christian even have any solid hope for a release of the constructive type of tension? We are not referring here to the ordinary worries and tensions of the average Christian. As suggested previously, these destructive tensions can be eliminated or reduced by a stronger faith in the Lord. The tension we have been concerned with and are talking about here is that which is greatest or strongest for sincere and mature Christians, for those who are most responsive to the will of God and the most sensitive to the leadership of the divine Spirit. Are there any sources of release for such tension which at times seems almost unbearable for the prophetic Christian?

One step in the release of constructive tension is a recognition that such tension is a natural and necessary part of creative living. Abraham Heschel says that "all that is creative stems from a seed of endless discontent." Such creative tension is an indication of growth or progress. Here we refer not only to progress for the individual Christian but also for his church and the society in which he lives. So long as we are maturing, which should be to the end of life, we should continue to search for the Holy Grail, for a better and higher way of life. Furthermore, a discontent with our present level of living and with the world in which we live, including our church, will move us in the direction of a deeper and more meaningful contentment than we could not have without such a movement.

There are some Christians, unfortunately, who seemingly are largely free from creative constructive tension simply because they close their eyes and minds to their own failures and shortcomings and to the problems of the world. They tend to see everything, including themselves, through rose-colored glasses. Or, if they are conscious of the moral and spiritual problems around them, they seek to convince themselves that the situation is more or less inevitable, that they cannot do anything about it. They adjust to or accept conditions as they are. They make their peace with the world. It is doubtful, however, if the Christian can indefinitely find peace within and with God through such a process or procedure.

Another step toward release is for the Christian to make an honest effort to apply fully the Christian spirit and ideal to his life and to the world. There can be no release from tension without some effort to improve or to remove the conditions that create the tension. The Christian will discover, however, that his efforts alone will not give him complete relief from tension. He may derive some satisfaction from the progress he makes toward the ideal, but it seems that the more progress he makes the deeper will be his consciousness that his best efforts fall far short of God's purpose for his life and for the world. In other words, the conscientious Christian cannot attain full release of or relief from the tensions of life through his own efforts.

Our Christian faith offers another means for the release of tension. That means is repentance. When we realize that we have failed, that we have fallen short of the purposes of God in our lives, we can cry unto him for forgiveness. We can do this in confidence, knowing that we have "an advocate with the Father, Jesus Christ the righteous" (1 John 2:1).

An abiding faith in God is still another means for the release of tension. We are not talking about a blind fatalism that will cause one to sit down and do nothing. Rather, we are talking about the kind of faith that will impel and inspire one to do the will of God as best he can and trust the Lord to take care of the results and also to take care of him. He believes that if he is on the side of the sovereign God of the universe, he is on the side of ultimate victory.

There is involved in the preceding one of the many paradoxes of our Christian faith. The serious Christian is never completely free from tension, but as a backdrop for the tension, he can have at the same time the peace that passeth understanding. Such a peace stems from the Christian's faith in a God who is sovereign, a faith that saves him from defeating fears and enables him to live creatively although insecurely in the world. Paul Tillich suggests that "yes" and "no" is a law of all truth. We can have the courage to accept the infinite tension between yes and no because "there is a yes above the yes and no of life and truth." This is a yes which is not ours. It is the resurrection of Christ that reveals "the final yes without another no."[4]

Continuance of Tension

As previously suggested, the serious Christian will never be completely free from tension. It could not be otherwise since the Christian at his best is always on the way, he is always becoming, he never fully attains. How could it be otherwise when his life is to be measured by the stature found in Christ?

Also, when the Christian repents of falling short of God's glory, of his will and purpose, and God forgives and restores him to fellowship, that renewed fellowship in turn gives him a clearer and deeper insight into God's will for his life and his purposes for the world. He receives a new vision from God. He then goes from the presence of the Lord and attempts to make that vision a reality in his life and in the world. He falls short. Again he repents. God forgives. He received a deepened insight into God's will for him and his world. This process is repeated over and over again.

The preceding may seem to represent a continuous meaningless paradoxical round. This is not the viewpoint, however, of the understanding Christian. It may be a round, but each round can and should represent some progress toward the Christian ideal, toward the intentional or ultimate will of God. The constant round is inevitable, since the final standard for the Christian is full maturity, completeness, wholeness, or perfection, and a wholeness or perfection found in God.

Tension is not only a continuing experience for the individual Christian but also for the Christian community. It is true that some churches have so completely made their peace with the world that there seems to be no tension between the church and the world. Such a church has lost its power to lift the world toward God's purposes for it. The message of such a church, however, is always superior to its practice. That message creates tension, to some degree, even within the worldly, secular church and between it and the world. The tension that should be felt between the church and the world will be strengthened and made more effective if it is created not only by what the church preaches but also by what it practices.

The tension between the church and the world should not become so great that the church would lose all opportunity to minister to the world and the people of the world. If we think of that tension as a rubber band, we may see more clearly what is meant. The degree to which the world is lifted toward the Christian ideal will be determined by the tautness of the "rubber band." On the other hand, if the tension becomes too great the "band" may break and the church would no longer be able to minister effectively to the world. The individual or the group, church or otherwise, that serves most effectively the world and the people of the world must progressively seek to move it and them toward the Christian ideal. This means that the Christian ideal for the individual and for the world is never static; it is always dynamic, always in movement. As we move toward it, it moves ahead of us.

Most of us and most of our churches do not need the preceding warning. The greater danger is that we and they will go entirely too far in adjusting the Christian ideal to the so-called "realities of life." Too frequently we tend to identify the ideal with what we consider the immediately attainable, to equate the circumstantial will of God with his intentional will. When the church does this, it will mean the loss of tension between the message it proclaims and the world. Such a church will tend to become conformed to the world rather than to be a transformer of the world.

FOR THOUGHT AND DISCUSSION

1. One source of tension for many young people and some older people is their relation to the institutional church. Some think that there is a conflict between their commitment to Christ and his cause in the world and their commitment or loyalty to the church. What suggestions would you make to one who is striving with that problem? Where do most of the insights come from that are used to criticize the institutional church? Will you agree that most of them have come from the message of the church which we must admit is preached better than it is practiced? How can one best influence the church: from outside or from within?

Would the "drop-outs" serve their cause better by "dropping-in"? Would this always be true or would it just be true on the part of some? What is your appraisal of your own church?

2. Most church groups have not worked out a generally acceptable position on the relation of church and state. This creates tension within the churches, within the Christian movement as such, and in society. What is your judgment concerning such related problems as taxation of church property, prayer and Bible reading in public schools, government aid to church-related schools?

3. There has been some tension in the contemporary period concerning the relative importance of law and order on the one hand and justice on the other. What do you think? Is the division of law and order and justice justified? Or does "law" belong as much with "justice" as with "order"? Would you agree that the three really belong together—that society cannot have order without justice as well as law? Which—"justice" or "order"—should receive priority in a time of rapid change or revolution? Why?

ANNOTATED BIBLIOGRAPHY

The emphasis will be on relatively recent publications. Some older titles will be included that have become more or less standard. A few out of print books (OP) will be listed. They are considered outstanding, with nothing comparable to them in contemporary publications. The selections will be restricted to publications in English.

I. GENERAL

Books in this group are of several types. Some are reference books. A few have been written for textbook purposes. Some represent distinctly denominational perspectives. Still others could be classified in more than one of the subsequent groups or would not fit under any of the other headings.

Barnette, Henlee H. *Introducing Christian Ethics.* Nashville: Broadman Press, 1961. Emphasis on biblical and social or applied ethics.

Curran, Charles E., ed. *Absolutes in Moral Theology.* Washington, Cleveland: Corpus Books, 1968. Another book by Curran, a teacher in the Roman Catholic University of America, is *A New Look at Christian Morality.* Notre Dame: Fides Publishers, Inc., 1968.

Dewar, Lindsay. *An Outline of Anglican Moral Theology.* London: Mowbray, 1968.

DeWolf, L. Harold. *Responsible Freedom: Guidelines for Christian Action.* New York: Harper & Row, 1971. An inclusive volume (336 pages) concerning ethics under two general headings: Part I, Basic Principles, and Part II, Applied Christian Ethics.

Gardner, E. Clinton. *Biblical Faith and Social Ethics.* New York: Harper & Brothers, 1960. Similar to Barnette in structure.

Gustafson, James M. *The Church as Moral-Decision Maker.* Philadelphia: Pilgrim Press, 1970. Essays previously published, selected by Charles M. Swezey, with a very helpful introduction by Swezey to Gustafson's writings in general.

Henry, Carl F. H. *Christian Personal Ethics.* Grand Rapids: Wm. B. Eerdmans Publishing Co., 1957. A comprehensive book (over 600 pages) by a leading conservative scholar.

Macquarrie, John, ed. *Dictionary of Christian Ethics.* Philadelphia: Westminster Press, 1967.

Macquarrie, John. *Three Issues in Ethics.* New York: Harper & Row, 1970. Seeks to answer three questions: (1) What are the theological grounds for cooperation between Christians and non-Christians on ethical matters? (2) What relevance does a religious faith have to moral life? (3) Is there a distinctly Christian ethic?

Mehl, Roger. *Catholic Ethics and Protestant Ethics.* Translated by James H. Farley. Philadelphia: Westminster Press, 1971. Suggests in the last of three chapters that the renewal of interest in the Bible and in social ethics in Catholic and Protestant circles is moving the two major religious groups closer together.

Pinson, William M., Jr. *Resource Guide to Current Social Issues.* Waco: Word Book, 1968. Arranged by subjects alphabetically; references to books, pamphlets, visual aids, and organizational sources for help.

Rauschenbusch, Walter. *A Theology for the Social Gospel.* New York: Macmillan Company, 1918. Other major books of Rauschenbusch are *Christianity and the Social Crisis* (1907) and *Christianizing the Social Order* (1912).

Smith, Harmon L., and Hodges, Louis W. *The Christian and His Decisions.* Nashville, New York: Abingdon Press, 1969. An introduction to Christian ethics. Two of the three major divisions are readings on theological foundations and principles of decision making. The third division, "The Practice of Christian Decision Making," is the work of the editors.

Thielicke, Helmut. *Theological Ethics.* Vol. I: *Foundations.* Edited by William H. Lazareth. Philadelphia: Fortress Press, 1966.

Tillich, Paul. *Morality and Beyond.* New York: Harper & Row, 1963. "How the moral is related to the religious."

Toews, Abraham P. *The Problem of Mennonite Ethics.* Grand Rapids: Wm. B. Eerdmans Publishing Co., 1963.

II. HISTORICAL

Beach, Waldo, and Niebuhr, H. Richard, eds. *Christian Ethics.* New York: Ronald Press, 1955. Selected readings from the Didache through Rauschenbusch with interpretative introductions. An introductory chapter on biblical ethics and a closing one, "Current Trends."

Cadoux, Cecil John. *The Early Church and the World.* Edinburgh: T. &. T. Clark, 1925 (OP). Restricted to first three centuries.

Hall, Thomas Cuming. *History of Ethics within Organized Christianity.* London: T. Fisher Unwin, 1910 (OP).

Handy, Robert T., ed. *The Social Gospel in America, 1870-1920.* New York: Oxford University Press, 1966. Compilation of papers of Washington Gladden, Richard T. Ely, and Walter Rauschenbusch with excellent introductions and editorial comments.

Harkness, Georgia Elma. *John Calvin: The Man and His Ethics.* New York: H. Holt and Co., 1931; Nashville: Abingdon, 1958, paper.

Hiers, Richard H. *Jesus and Ethics.* Philadelphia: Westminster Press, 1968. An examination of "Ethics without Eschatology" (Harnack), "Ethics and Eschatology" (Schweitzer), "Ethics as Eschatology" (Bultmann), and "The Ethics of Realized Eschatology" (Dodd).

Kirk, Kenneth E. *The Vision of God.* New York: Longmans, Green and Co., 1932 (OP). The summum bonum is the vision of God or worship.

Troeltsch, Ernst. *The Social Teaching of the Christian Churches.* 2 vols. Translated by Olive Wyon. New York: Macmillan Company, 1931. Available in paper.

III. BIBLICAL

Alexander, Archibald B. D. *The Ethics of St. Paul.* Glasgow: Maclehose and Sons, 1910 (OP).

Enslin, Morton Scott. *The Ethics of Paul.* New York: Harper & Brothers, Publishers, 1930; paper, 1957.

Furnish, Victor Paul. *The Theology and Ethics in Paul.* Nashville: Abingdon Press, 1968. Scholarly. Emphasis on ethics but Paul's ethics "radically integral to his basic theological convictions."

Knox, John. *The Ethic of Jesus in the Teaching of the Church.* New York: Abingdom Press, 1961. Discusses the distinctly Christian ethic and particularly problems that are created when it is taken seriously.

Lillie, William. *Studies in New Testament Ethics.* Edinburgh: Oliver and Boyd, 1961. Subject oriented.

Manson, T. W. *Ethics and the Gospel.* New York: Charles Scribner's Sons, 1960.

Marshall, L. II. *The Challenge of New Testament Ethics.* London: Macmillan and Co., Ltd., 1946. Restricted to Jesus and Paul.

Maston, T. B. *Biblical Ethics.* Waco: Word Books, 1967. A survey majoring on biblical content. A chapter on Apocrypha, Pseudepigrapha, and Dead Sea Scrolls.

Muilenburg, James. *The Way of Israel.* New York: Harper & Brothers, 1961. Subtitle: "Biblical Faith and Ethics."

Nygren, Anders. *Agape and Eros.* Rev. ed. Translated by Philip S. Watson. London: SPCK, 1953; also paper, 1969.

Wilder, Amos Niven. *Eschatology and Ethics in the Teaching of Jesus.* Rev. ed. New York: Harper, 1950. Also a booklet (38 pages) *Kerygma, Eschatology, and Social Ethics.* Philadelphia: Fortress Press, 1966.

IV. BASIC

These are books that major on one or more basic concepts or principles.

Bonhoeffer, Dietrich, *Ethics.* Edited by Eberhard Bethge. New York: Macmillan Company, 1955. A number of other books by this creative writer. One of the most directly helpful is *The Cost of Discipleship* (1937).

Brunner, Emil. *The Divine Imperative. A Study in Christian Ethics.* Translated by Olive Wyon. London: Lutterworth Press, 1937. Still stands as one of the major books, particularly Books I and II.

Carpenter, Edward. *Common Sense about Christian Ethics.* New York: Macmillan Company, 1961. Practical, helpful, relatively simple, no documentation.

Ellul, Jacques. *To Will and to Do.* Translated by C. Edward Hopkin. Philadelphia: Pilgrim Press, 1969. Revelational in emphasis. Third and last major division on "The Impossibility and the Necessity of a Christian Ethic" particularly challenging.

Gustafson, James M. *Christ and the Moral Life.* New York: Harper & Row, Publishers, 1968. One of the outstanding books in recent years.

Lehmann, Paul. *Ethics in a Christian Context.* New York: Harper & Row, Publishers, 1963. Emphasis on a *koinonia* ethic and on the contextual nature of ethics.

Long, Edward LeRoy, Jr. *A Survey of Christian Ethics.* New York: Oxford University Press, 1967. Historical in perspective; organized around certain motifs.

Muelder, Walter G. *Moral Law in Christian Social Ethics.* Richmond: John Knox Press, 1966. An attempt to vindicate moral laws. An examination and updating, in the main, of the *Moral Laws* suggested by Brightman about thirty years ago.

Niebuhr, H. Richard. *The Responsible Self; an essay in Christian moral philosophy* with an introduction by James M. Gustafson. New York: Harper & Row, 1963. Published after the author's death. Gustafson's introduction of approximately 35 pages is an excellent review of Niebuhr's books and thought.

Niebuhr, Reinhold. *The Nature and Destiny of Man: A Christian Interpretiaton.* 2 vols. New York: Charles Scribner's Sons, 1941. Also paper. Vol. I on the Nature of Man particularly helpful.

Oden, Thomas C. *Radical Obedience; the ethics of Rudolph Bultmann, with a response by Rudolf Bultmann.* Philadelphia: Westminster Press, 1964.

Outka, Gene H., and Ramsey, Paul, eds. *Norm and Context in Christian Ethics.* New York: Charles Scribner's Sons, 1968. Also paper. An effort "to assess the place of norms in religious ethics." Representative contributors.

V. APPLIED OR SOCIAL

Only general books will be included. Those on specific areas, such as family, race, etc., are so many and are out of date so soon that it was not considered wise to include them.

Gustafson, James M., and Laney, James T., eds. *On Being Responsible: Issues in Personal Ethics.* New York: Harper & Row, 1968. Paper. A book of readings. After an introductory section the main subject headings are on being responsible in speech, in love, and in citizenship.

Letts, Harold C., ed. *Christian Social Responsibility.* A symposium in three volumes. Philadelphia: Muhlenberg Press, 1957. Vol. III on *Life in Community* will be most helpful.

Maston, T. B. *Christianity and World Issues.* New York: Macmillan Company, 1957. Deals rather thoroughly with a few of the major issues.

Maston, T. B. *The Christian, the Church, and Contemporary Problems.* Waco: Word Books, 1968. Collection of articles and addresses, topically organized.

Rasmussen, Albert Terrill. *Christian Social Ethics.* Englewood Cliffs, N. J.: Prentice-Hall, Inc., 1956. The subtitle, "Exerting Christian Influence," suggests the main thrust of the book.

Sellers, James. *Public Ethics: American Morals and Manners.* New
    York: Harper & Row, Publishers, 1970. Two major divi-
    sions: I. Toward a Theory of Public Ethics; II. The Role
    of Theology in Public Ethics.

VI. RELATION TO CULTURE

Beach, Waldo. *Christian Community and American Society.* Phila-
    delphia: Westminster Press, 1969. An effort to engage the
    Christian theologian and the social scientist in dialogue.
Bennett, John C., ed. *Christian Social Ethics in a Changing World.*
    New York: Association Press, 1966. Sub-title: "An Ec-
    umenical Theological Inquiry." Chapters vary considera-
    bly in value.
Duff, Edward. *The Social Thought of the World Council of
    Churches.* New York: Association Press, 1956.
Gardner, E. Clinton. *The Church as a Prophetic Community.* Phil-
    adelphia: Westminster Press, 1967. If the church is to find
    renewal and to be relevant to contemporary culture, it
    must understand that it is a prophetic community.
Gilkey, Langdon. *How the Church Can Minister to the World
    without Losing Itself.* New York: Harper & Row, 1964.
    Primarily interested in churches or denominations that
    stand between church-type and sect-type. Discusses under
    three main symbols: The People of God, Hearers of the
    Word, and Body of Christ.
Gottwald, Norman K. *The Church Unbound.* Philadelphia: J. B.
    Lippincott Co., 1967. On "church-culture interaction"
    with biblical and historical background.
Gustafson, James M. *Treasure in Earthen Vessels: The Church as
    a Human Community.* New York: Harper & Brothers,
    1961. The church is a divine-human institution. Gustafson
    concentrates on its human nature. As a human or natural
    institution strictly human approaches can be helpful in a
    study of the church.
Niebuhr, H. Richard. *Christ and Culture.* New York: Harper &
    Brothers, 1951. Also paper. A classic.

VII. SITUATION ETHICS

Because of the current interest in situation ethics it was considered wise to include some of the better books on the subject.

Barr, O. Sydney. *The Christian New Morality*. New York: Oxford University Press, 1969. The subtitle describes the distinctive emphasis of the book: "A Biblical Study of Situation Ethics." Concentrates on love in the life and teachings of Jesus, in Pauline epistles, and in the Johannine literature.

Bennett, John C., *et al. Storm over Ethics*. United Church Press, 1967. Closing chapter, "Situation Ethics under Fire," is by Fletcher.

Cox, Harvey, ed. *The Situation Ethics Debate*. Philadelphia: Westminster Press, 1968. Composed of letters, reviews, and appraisals in articles and books by many authors. Fletcher replies in closing chapter.

Dunphy, William, ed. *The New Morality: Continuity and Discontinuity*. New York: Herder and Herder, 1967. Main value the biblical and historical background.

Fletcher, Joseph Francis. *Moral Responsibility*. Philadelphia: Westminster Press, 1967. A reproduction, in the main, of previously published articles and lectures. The most significant is "The New Look in Christian Ethics," published in the "Harvard Divinity Bulletin," which sets forth the six propositions that provide the foundation for and direction of situation ethics.

Fletcher, Joseph Francis. *Situation Ethics*. Philadelphia: Westminster Press, 1966. Paper. The one necessary book for an understanding of situation ethics.

Fletcher, Joseph F., and Wassmer, Thomas. *Hello, Lovers*. Edited by William E. May. Washington: Corpus Books, 1970. A dialogue between Fletcher and Wassmer, a Jesuit moralist and teacher.

Ramsey, Paul. *Deeds and Rules in Christian Ethics*. New York: Charles Scribner's Sons, 1967. Paper. Includes an analysis

or review of the "Honest to God" debate, Paul Lehmann's
contextualism, and Fletcher's situationalism.
Robinson, John A. T. *Christian Morals Today.* Philadelphia:
Westminster Press, 1964. Paper. Booklet of 47 pages.

NOTES

I. INTRODUCTION: MAN'S SEARCH FOR TRUTH

[1] John Calvin, *Institutes of the Christian Religion*, trans. by J. Beveridge (James Clarke & Co., 1949), II, 4.

[2] Paul L. Lehmann, *Ethics in a Christian Context* (Harper & Row, 1963), p. 25.

II. THE NATURE OF GOD

[1] Augustine, *Confessions,* (Everyman's Library), p. 99.

[2] Dietrich Bonhoeffer, *Letters and Papers from Prison* (SCM Press, 1963), p. 93. Some reputable scholars have misused or at best used Bonhoeffer "one-sidedly." Thomas Oden says that "Bonhoeffer is in most respects a Barthian who asked embarrassing questions" (*Radical Obedience*, Westminster Press, 1964, p. 22). Many of those questions were asked in his letters from prison, frequently when he was thinking out loud. Unfortuantely, some people have used these questions along with statements in those letters without proper regard for Bonhoeffer's over-all perspective. He has been claimed as a supporter of almost every conceivable position, some of which I am persuaded would be highly embarrassing to him.

[3] John Calvin, *Institutes of the Christian Religion,* II, 4.

III. THE NATURE OF MAN

[1] Karl Barth, *Church Dogmatics*, trans. by A. T. Mackay, *et al.* (T. & T. Clark, 1961), III, 4, 117.

IV. THE BIBLICAL REVELATION

[1] For a few examples see Matt. 22:24; Mark 7:10; 12:19; Luke 20:28; Acts 3:22; Rom. 10:5, 19; and for similar references to Isaiah see Matt. 15:7; Mark 7:6; John 1:23; and Rom. 12:29.

² See H. H. Rowley, *The Unity of the Bible* (Carey Kingsgate Press, 1953), p. 7, and his *The Faith of Israel* (SCM Press, 1950), p. 14.

³ H. Wheeler Robinson, *Religious Ideas of the Old Testament* (9th impression; Gerald Duckworth and Co., 1952), p. 225.

⁴ G. Ernest Wright, *The Old Testament against Its Environment* (Henry Regnery, 1950), pp. 111–12.

⁵ Bonhoeffer, *Letters and Papers from Prison*, p. 103.

V. THE CHRISTIAN EXPERIENCE

¹ Adolf Deissmann, *The Religion of Jesus and the Faith of Paul*, trans. by William E. Wilson (2d ed.; Hodder & Stoughton, 1926), p. 171. An earlier and equally important book of Deissmann's was *St. Paul: A Study in Social and Religious History*, trans. by Lionel R. M. Strachan (Hodder & Stoughton, 1912). Two books that accept and utilize the mystical interpretation of "in Christ," which was first popularized by Deissman, are James S. Stewart, *A Man in Christ* (Harper, 1935), and William Barclay, *The Mind of St. Paul* (Harper, 1958).

² John's well-known triology of favorite words are life, light, and love. In addition to "abide" another that should be added to the list is "send" or "sent," which is found more frequently in the gospel of John than any other of his generally recognized favorite words.

³ Paul Lehmann, *Ethics in a Christian Concept*, p. 131.

⁴ Helmut Thielicke, *Theological Ethics* (Fortress Press, 1966), I, 93.

⁵ Søren Kierkegaard, *Training in Christianity*, trans. by Walter Lowrie (Oxford University Press, 1941), p. 234.

⁶ Søren Kierkegaard, *Purity of Heart*, trans. by Douglas V. Steere (Harper, 1938, 1948), p. 202.

⁷ *Ibid.*, p. 293.

⁸ Calvin, *Institutes*, II, 5.

⁹ Dietrich Bonhoeffer, *The Cost of Discipleship*, trans. by R. H. Fuller (SCM Press, 1948), p. 111.

¹⁰ For other visions that included a command to do some-

thing for God and his people, see Ex. 3:1–12 (Moses), 1 Sam. 3:1–14 (Samuel), 1 Kings 19:1–18 (Elijah), and Acts 10:1–48 (Peter).

[11] John A. T. Robinson, *Honest to God* (Westminster Press, 1963), p. 90.

VI. ITS HIGHEST MOTIVE: GLORY TO GOD

[1] The following will be helpful if you wish to do general reading concerning the glory of God: Bernard Ramm, *Them He Glorified* (Eerdmans, 1963), the subtitle describes the nature of the book—*A Systematic Study of the Doctrine of Glorification*; Arthur Michael Ramsey, *The Glory of God and the Transfiguration* (Longmans, Green, 1949), approximately two-thirds of this book is a scholarly, compact study of "glory" in both Testaments. Excellent articles will be found in some of the Bible dictionaries and in Bible helps such as J.-J. Von Allmen (ed.), *A Companion to the Bible* (Oxford University Press, 1958).

[2] Von Allmen, *A Companion to the Bible*, p. 137.

[3] Alan Richardson (ed.), *A Theological Word Book of the Bible* (Macmillan, 1950), p. 202.

[4] Gerhard Kittel (ed.), *Theological Dictionary of the New Testament*, trans. and ed. by Geoffrey W. Bromiley (Eerdmans, 1967), IV, 715.

[5] C. S. Lewis, *The Weight of Glory* (Macmillan, 1949), p. 2.

[6] Edward Carpenter, *Common Sense about Christian Ethics* (Macmillan, 1961), p. 61.

[7] Ramsey, p. 54.

[8] Von Allmen, p. 139.

[9] Ramsey, p. 92.

VII. ITS ULTIMATE AUTHORITY: THE WILL OF GOD

[1] Paul Tillich, *Morality and Beyond* (Harper & Row, 1963), pp. 34–35.

[2] Henlee H. Barnette, *Introducing Christian Ethics* (Broadman Press, 1961), p. 94.

³ Emil Brunner, *The Divine Imperative*, trans. by Olive Wyon (Lutterworth Press, 1937), p. 92.

⁴ One of the most evident weaknesses of situation ethics is the limited place given to the Holy Spirit. For example, the index to Joseph Fletcher's *Situation Ethics* (Westminster Press, 1966), has only four references to the Holy Spirit. One is a quotation from Paul, while in two places he equates the Holy Spirit and love: "Love is not the work of the Holy Spirit, it *is* the Holy Spirit—working in us" (p. 51, cf. p. 155).

⁵ John Knox, *Criticism and Faith* (Abingdon-Cokesbury Press, 1952), p. 63.

⁶ See pp. 57–59 for a discussion of the relevance of the Bible.

⁷ Of many books on or reflective of situation ethics, the one best book is Joseph Fletcher's *Situation Ethics*. John A. T. Robinson has a chapter (6) entitled "The New Morality" in his *Honest to God*. He later published a booklet of approximately fifty pages entitled *Christian Morals Today* (Westminster Press, 1964). Two books with multiple authors which examine the pros and cons of situation ethics are: *Storm over Ethics* (Bethany Press, 1967), and particularly Harvey Cox (ed.), *The Situation Ethics Debate* (Westminister Press, 1968). No one has been sharper or more vocal in his criticism of situation ethics and particularly Fletcher than Paul Ramsey. This is seen in his *Deeds and Rules in Christian Ethics* (Scribner's, 1967) in which a chapter is devoted to the Honest to God debate and another to "The Case of Joseph Fletcher and Joseph Fletcher's Cases."

⁸ Emil Brunner, *The Divine Imperative*, p. 83.

⁹ Karl Barth, *Church Dogmatics*, trans. by G. W. Bromiley, *et al.* (T. & T. Clark, 1957), II, 2, 701.

¹⁰ William Barclay, *The Gospel of Matthew* (Westminster Press, 2nd ed., 1958), II, 97.

VIII. ITS SUPREME VALUE: THE KINGDOM OF GOD

¹ Two of the better recent books on the kingdom of God are George Eldon Ladd, *Jesus and the Kingdom* (Harper & Row, 1964), and Norman Perrin, *The Kingdom of God in the Teaching of Jesus* (Westminster Press, 1963). Ladd's book is more thorough

than his earlier book, *The Gospel of the Kingdom* (Eerdmans, 1959). Perrin's book, in the main, is an analysis of the position of various scholars concerning the kingdom.

Three of the most helpful older books on the kingdom are John Bright, *The Kingdom of God* (Abingdon, 1953); H. Richard Niebuhr, *The Kingdom of God in America* (Willett, Clark, and Co., 1937); and Ernest F. Scott, *The Kingdom of God in the New Testament* (Macmillan, 1931).

Martin Buber's *Kingship of God*, trans. by Richard Scheimann (Harper & Row, 1967), provides some background material for an understanding of the kingdom concept. Based on a manuscript discovered after his death, Albert Schweitzer's *The Kingdom of God and Primitive Christianity*, trans. by L. A. Garrard (Seabury Press, 1968), is a survey of biblical material, with a major emphasis on the teachings of Jesus.

[2] The phrase "kingdom of God" is seldom found outside of the synoptics. There are only two references in John (3:3, 5), six in Acts, and a total of only eight in all the Pauline epistles, with five of these in First Corinthians. It is possible that Paul avoided the use of an expression so predominantly Jewish in its background. It has been suggested that "eternal life" in John's writings, and to a lesser degree in the Pauline epistles, is comparable to "kingdom" in the synoptics. There are sixteen specific references to "eternal life" in John's gospel with an additional six in First John.

[3] Most books on the kingdom, such as Bright, Ladd, and Schweitzer, give considerable attention to the Jewish background for the kingdom of God. Rudolf Schnackenburg, *God's Rule and Kingdom* (Herder & Herder, 1963), devotes the first of three major divisions to "The Kingship of God in the Old Testament and in Later Judaism."

[4] Bright, *The Kingdom of God*, p. 216.

[5] Wolfhart Pannenberg, *Theology and the Kingdom of God* (Westminster Press, 1969), p. 53.

[6] L. H. Marshall, *The Challenge of New Testament Ethics* (Macmillan, 1946), p. 31.

[7] Karl Barth, *Church Dogmatics*, trans. by G. W. Bromiley and R. J. Ehrlich (T. & T. Clark, 1960), III, 3, 157.

[8] *Ibid.*, IV, 2, 655–56.

[9] See Amos N. Wilder's *Eschatology and Ethics in the Teaching of Jesus* (rev. ed.; Harper & Brothers, 1958). Considerable material in the book relates to the kingdom, with the last two chapters most specifically on the kingdom: "The Ethics of the Kingdom and the Mission of Jesus" and "The Kingdom of God and Moral Life."

[10] T. B. Maston, *Biblical Ethics* (Word Books, 1967), pp. 51–52.

[11] Pannenberg, p. 73. Ladd, in his *Jesus and the Kingdom*, has a chapter (11) on "The Kingdom and the Church." The discussion is built around five points, which summarize his position: (1) The church is not the kingdom. (2) The kingdom creates the church. (3) The church witnesses to the kingdom. (4) The church is the instrument of the kingdom. (5) The church: the custodian of the kingdom.

[12] Paul Tillich, *Love, Power, and Justice* (Oxford University Press, 1954), p. 134.

IX. ITS COMPREHENSIVE IDEAL: PERFECTION

[1] Helmut Thielicke, 1, 486.

[2] John Wesley, *A Plain Account of Christian Perfection* (Epworth Press, 1952), p. 41; cf. pp. 42, 43.

[3] *Ibid.*, p. 17.

[4] R. Newton Flew, *The Idea of Perfection in Christian Theology* (Oxford University Press, 1934), p. 52.

[5] *Ibid.*, p. 5.

[6] See Thielicke, pp. 152–53.

[7] T. W. Manson, *The Sayings of Jesus* (SCM Press, 1949), p. 9.

[8] E. J. Tinsley, *The Imitation of God in Christ* (Westminster Press, 1960), p. 150.

[9] *Ibid.*, p. 134. Tinsley quotes the following scriptures: 1 Thess. 2:12; 4:1, 12; 2 Thess. 3:6, 11; 1 Cor. 7:17; 2 Cor. 4:2; 5:7; 10:3; 12:18; Gal. 6:16; Rom. 6:4; 8:4; 13:13; 14:15; Eph. 2:10; 4:1; 5:2; Phil. 3:17; Col. 1:10; 2:6; 4:5. There are other references to the "way" in Paul such as "a still more excellent way" of *agape* (1 Cor. 12:31). A good concordance will reveal many more references to the way including "the way of the Lord" quite prominent

in the Old Testament (see Deut. 8:6; 10:12; 28:9; 2 Kings 21:22; Prov. 2:13; 14:2; 28:26; Isa. 33:15; 38:3).

[10] Thielicke, p. 131.

[11] Flew, p. 6.

[12] Calvin, *Institutes*, II, 5.

X. ITS CROWNING VIRTUE: LOVE

[1] Karl Barth, *Church Dogmatics*, trans. by Harold Knight, *et al.* (T. & T. Clark, 1960), III, 2, 279.

[2] The standard work, under considerable criticism in recent years, on *eros* and *agape* is Anders Nygren, *Agape and Eros*, trans. by Philip S. Watson (rev. ed.; S.P.C.K., 1963). Barth in a number of places compares *eros* and *agape*. For a helpful and rather lengthy discussion, see *Church Dogmatics*, IV, 2, 733–51. Edward LeRoy Long, Jr., *A Survey of Christian Ethics* (Oxford University Press, 1967), pp. 138–43, has a helpful, compact analysis and appraisal of Nygren. For an examination of every use of *agapon, agape,* and *agapetos* in the New Testament, see the three volumes by Ceslaus Spicq, *Agape in the New Testament*, trans. by Marie Aquinas McNamara and Mary Honoria Richter (B. Herder Book Co., 1963–66).

[3] Emil Brunner, *Justice and the Social Order*, trans. by Mary Hottinger (Lutterworth Press, 1945), p. 114.

[4] Fletcher, *Situation Ethics*, p. 61.

[5] Maston, *Biblical Ethics*, pp. 206–7.

[6] Barth, *Church Dogmatics*, I, 2, 371.

[7] Fletcher, *Situation Ethics*, p. 87.

[8] Paul Tillich, *The New Being* (Scribner's, 1955), p. 33.

[9] Reinhold Niebuhr, *The Nature and Destiny of Man* (Scribner's, 1943), II, 246.

[10] Emil Brunner, *Justice and the Social Order*, p. 117.

[11] Fletcher, *Situation Ethics,* p. 74.

[12] Søren Kierkegaard, *Works of Love*, trans. by David F. Swenson and Lillian Marvin Swenson (Princeton University Press, 1946), p. 87. Douglas Steere, in his introduction, says that this book is Kierkegaard's "greatest single work on Christian ethics."

[13] John A. T. Robinson, *Christian Morals Today*, p. 21.

[14] Kierkegaard, *Works of Love,* pp. 85–87.

[15] Paul Tillich, *Morality and Beyond* (Harper & Row, 1963), p. 93.

[16] Barth, *Church Dogmatics,* IV, 1, 106.

[17] Martin Luther, "On the Sum of the Christian Life," in *Luther's Works,* ed. and trans. by John W. Doberstein (Muhlenberg Press, 1959), LI, 269.

[18] Calvin, *Institutes,* I, 358.

XI. ITS UNIFYING GOAL: THE CROSS

[1] Douglas Webster, *In Debt to Christ* (Fortress Press, 1957), p. 12.

[2] Karl Barth, *Church Dogmatics,* IV, 2, 605.

[3] *Ibid.,* p. 604.

[4] Dietrich Bonhoeffer, *The Cost of Discipleship,* p. 73.

[5] Emil Brunner, *The Divine Imperative,* p. 175.

[6] W. T. Conner, *The Gospel of Redemption* (Broadman Press, 1945), p. 130.

[7] The expression "the cross of Christ" is found only in Paul's epistles (see 1 Cor. 1:17; Gal. 6:23, 14; and Phil. 3:18) with several additional references to "the cross" (see 1 Cor. 1:18; Gal. 5:11; Eph. 2:16; Phil. 2:8; Col. 1:20; 2:14). The only other specific reference to the cross outside of the gospels is Hebrews 12:2.

[8] Bonhoeffer, *The Cost of Discipleship,* p. 71.

[9] *Ibid.,* p. 73.

XII. ITS CONTINUING PROBLEM: TENSION

[1] Walther Eichrodt, "The Question of Property in the Light of the Old Testament," *Biblical Authority for Today,* ed. by Alan Richardson and Wolfgang Schweitzer (SCM Press, 1951), p. 273.

[2] T. B. Maston, *Christianity and World Issues* (Macmillan, 1957), p. 350.

[3] Most of this section and the next one on "Continuance of Tension" are adaptations of material in my book on *Christianity and World Issues,* pp. 351–54.

[4] Paul Tillich, *The New Being,* pp. 102–3.